This book belongs to

....

The Word Snoop

Ursula Dubosarsky

THE WORD SNOOP

Illustrated by Tohby Riddle

Dial Books

First published in the United States 2009 by DIAL BOOKS
A member of Penguin Group (USA) Inc.
Published by The Penguin Group
Penguin Group (USA) Inc., 375 Hudson Street, New York, NY 10014, U.S.A. •
Penguin Group (Canada), 90 Eglinton Avenue East, Suite 700, Toronto, Ontario,
Canada M4P 2Y3 (a division of Pearson Penguin Canada Inc.) • Penguin
Books Ltd, 80 Strand, London WC2R 0RL, England • Penguin Ireland, 25 St.
Stephen's Green, Dublin 2, Ireland (a division of Penguin Books Ltd) • Penguin
Group (Australia), 250 Camberwell Road, Camberwell, Victoria 3124, Australia
(a division of Pearson Australia Group Pty Ltd) • Penguin Books India Pvt Ltd,
11 Community Centre, Panchsheel Park, New Delhi - 110 017, India • Penguin
Group (NZ), 67 Apollo Drive, Rosedale, North Shore 0632, New Zealand (a
division of Pearson New Zealand Ltd) • Penguin Books (South Africa) (Pty) Ltd,
24 Sturdee Avenue, Rosebank, Johannesburg 2196, South Africa • Penguin Books
Ltd, Registered Offices: 80 Strand, London WC2R 0RL, England

Published in Australia 2008 by Viking as *The Word Spy*

The publisher does not have any control over and does not assume any
responsibility for author or third-party websites or their content.

Text set in Adobe Caslon • Printed in the U.S.A.

1 3 5 7 9 10 8 6 4 2

Library of Congress Cataloging-in-Publication Data
Dubosarsky, Ursula, date.
The word snoop / Ursula Dubosarsky ; illustrated by Tohby Riddle.
p. cm.
Previously published under title: The word spy, 2008.
Summary: A tour of the English language from the beginning of the
alphabet in 4000 BC to modern text messaging and emoticons.
ISBN 978-0-8037-3406-7
1. English language—History—Juvenile literature. I. Riddle, Tohby,
ill. II. Duborsarsky, Ursula, date, Word spy. III. Title.
PE1075.D83 2009
420.9—dc22
2009008306

Polonius: *What do you read, my lord?*

Hamlet: *Words, words, words.*

HAMLET BY WILLIAM SHAKESPEARE

Dear Readers,

You may not know me, but I know you. I am—
the WORD SNOOP!

The Word Snoop? Allow me to explain . . . You
see, I love words. Ever since I can remember, I've
been listening to, speaking, reading, writing, and
yes—snooping on words. I follow words everywhere. I creep down dark hallways, roam wide
highways, and sneak along country lanes.
I listen to conversations, read over people's
shoulders, flip through books, click on
websites, and tap out text messages . . .

But the time has come at last for me to emerge
from undercover and share with you some of the
many, many things I have learned.

Why don't you come and be a Word Snoop with
me? All you have to do is open this book, take
a deep breath, and dive inside. The wonderful
world of words awaits!

But *shhh!* Someone's coming! I cannot stay.
See you very soon, I hope. Don't delay, my
snoops, I'm expecting you . . .

Bye-bye! Must fly!
Yours ever,

The Word Snoop

P.S. Oops, I almost forgot! There's a secret message for you hidden in the pages of this book. You will find a part of the message at the end of each chapter, and each part is written in its own special code.
See if you can decipher them all.
Farewell, my snoops . . . and good luck!

Contents

1. How it all began . . .

The First Alphabet **3**

The English Alphabet **9**

Let's Change the Alphabet **12**

Invent your own Alphabet **15**

Shorthand **18**

2. Why is English so strange?

Silent Letters **25**

The Invention of Printing **29**

American Spelling **35**

Plurals **39**

Hooray for Anglo-Saxon! **43**

Shakespeare and the Bible **46**

3. Dots and dashes, interrobangs and cat's claws

Punctuation **55**

Punctuation: Signs & Symbols **56**

Comma, colon: period. **57**

Question mark **58**   Exclamation mark **58**

Interrobang **59**

Quotation marks **60**   Apostrophe **61**
Punctuation in Other Languages **62**
Punctuation: Do we Need it? **65**

4. Letters, letters, letters
Anagrams **77**   Pangrams **81**
Lipograms **84**   Acronyms **88**
LLL (Latin, Latin, Latin) **94**
Well-mannered acronyms **95**
Dot dot dot **96**
And finally the backronym . . . **96**

5. Is that another Greek word?
Palindromes **105**
Mnemonics **110**
Oxymorons **113**

6. Who likes playing games?
Pig Latin **123**
The Rebus **127**
Rhyming Slang **131**

7. Say that again!
Puns **139**   Homophones **142**
Mondegreens **145**   Onomatopoeia **149**

Tongue Twisters **154**

Portmanteau Words **158**

8. Hmm, I wonder what you're really saying . . .

Euphemisms **169**

Don't Mention It **172**

Doublespeak **176**

Clichés **180**

Tautology **183**

9. Is that a real person?

Nicknames **195**   Eponyms **198**

Spoonerisms **200**

Tom Swifties **204**

Malapropisms **207**

Pen Names **212**

10. Back to the future

Telegramese **221**

Texting, LOL, Leet and More **225**

Smileys **228**

Glossary **236**

Keys **243**

Timeline

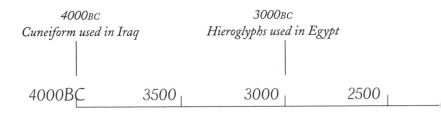

4000BC
Cuneiform used in Iraq

3000BC
Hieroglyphs used in Egypt

4000BC   3500   3000   2500

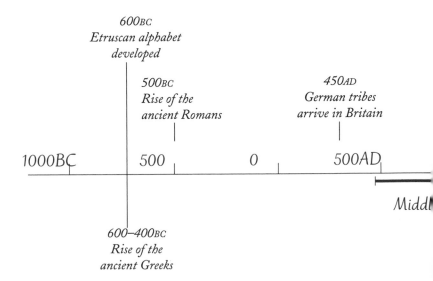

600BC
Etruscan alphabet
developed

500BC
Rise of the
ancient Romans

450AD
German tribes
arrive in Britain

1000BC   500   0   500AD

Middl

600–400BC
Rise of the
ancient Greeks

1500BC
Phoenician alphabet
developed

| 2000 | 1500 | 1000 |

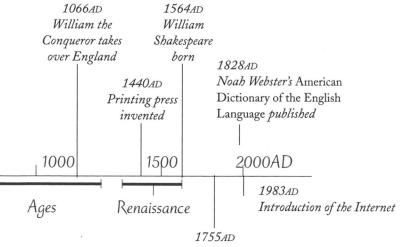

1066AD
William the
Conqueror takes
over England

1564AD
William
Shakespeare
born

1440AD
Printing press
invented

1828AD
Noah Webster's American
Dictionary of the English
Language *published*

| 1000 | 1500 | 2000AD |

Ages

Renaissance

1983AD
Introduction of the Internet

1755AD
Dr. Johnson's A Dictionary of
the English Language *published*

Dear Snoops,

I'm writing to you from a secret location. Don't tell anyone where I am, okay? Oh, that's right, you don't actually know where I am—do you?

Anyway, one thing you do know is your ABCs. That's right, the alphabet. Now, maybe the alphabet sounds like a pretty ordinary thing to you, but actually it's not. The only way you are able to read this book, or have it read to you, is because of the invention thousands of years ago of that mysterious thing we call—
The Alphabet.

It's funny, when something is as familiar as the alphabet you would think it had been there since the beginning of time. But it hasn't . . .

Read on, my friends!
And remember, keep snooping.

Your abecedarian friend,

The Word Snoop

1.
How
it all
began...

The First Alphabet

Imagine yourself back when you were learning the alphabet for the very first time. Twenty-six different letters—you probably thought you'd never be able to remember them all. But have you ever wondered where those strange shapes came from in the first place?

The very earliest writing in the world started in the area now known as Iraq in about 4000 BC. It's called cuneiform, which means "wedge-shaped." You know when you play with putty or clay, and you dig your fingernails into it to make shapes? Cuneiform was a bit like that—it was a way of writing by pressing wedges into soft clay to make signs for words and sounds. It looked like this:

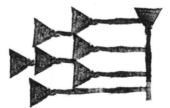

In ancient Egypt they did something a bit different. They carved or drew little pictures to show sounds or ideas. This kind of writing is called hieroglyphs, which means "holy writing" because it was mostly used by priests. Here's an example of a hieroglyph:

Can you guess what the word means? (I'll give you a hint—look at the very last picture. Meow!)

But neither cuneiform nor hieroglyphs were really alphabets. In an alphabet like ours, the signs or letters are supposed to stand only for sounds. To write the word *cat*, we use three letters to show those three sounds: **c a t**. But in writing systems like cuneiform and hieroglyphs, only some of the signs stood for sounds, while others stood for ideas or whole words, and sometimes these were combined (like the word for cat above—the first three pictures stand for sounds, while the last picture sums up the whole word). That sort of writing is a lot more complicated to write and to remember than an alphabet—in cuneiform alone there were about 1,500 different combinations!

The Phoenicians, who lived north of Egypt as far up as modern-day Lebanon and Syria, are said to be the first people who used an actual alphabet. It looked like this:

The first two letters of the Phoenician alphabet were called "aleph" and "beth." (Get it? Aleph-beth—Alphabet!) There were 22 letters, all consonants. Ys, thts rght, jst cnsnnts . . . The first letter, aleph, was not actually an A as we know it, but a funny sort of glugging sound in the throat. (Okay, you can stop glugging now.)

Anyway, because it made life simpler and writing quicker and easier, the Phoenician alphabet started to catch on, glug and all. The ancient Hebrew alphabet that most of the Bible was first written in is based on the Phoenician alphabet. The ancient Greeks adopted it too, adding extra letters for the vowels in around 1000 BC. (Phw! Tht ws lcky!) This is what the Greek alphabet looked like:

α β γ δ ε ζ η θ ι κ λ μ ν
ξ ο π ρ σ τ υ φ χ ψ ω

This alphabet eventually turned into the alphabet for Russian, Bulgarian, and other languages in that part of the world. In Italy, though, the Greek alphabet was adapted by the Etruscans, an amazing ancient people who lived in Italy before even the Romans did. This is how the Etruscans wrote their letters. (Are some of these starting to look familiar?)

The Romans got hold of the Etruscan alphabet, changed it a bit, and used it to write their language, Latin. It's more or less this Roman alphabet that we use to write English today—and French and Spanish and Italian and lots and lots of other languages as well. In fact, the Roman alphabet is now the most widely used alphabet in the world. Have you ever looked at the names of the fonts on your computer? One of the most popular fonts is called Roman—and now you know why!

So you thought kindergarten was hard . . .

It probably took you a while to learn the 26 letters of the alphabet back when you started school. But actually, you should count yourself lucky. Some languages use alphabets with many more letters than that. Russian, for example, has 33 letters, and the Khmer language of Cambodia has over 70. And in China and Japan, where they write with signs called characters, there are hundreds, even thousands of different shapes to remember. Japanese primary school children are expected to learn about a thousand characters before they can go on to high school!

Okay. But why do we use a Roman alphabet for writing in English? Why don't we have an English alphabet? Well, that's exactly what the Word Snoop wondered too, so I waited until it was dark, and then I crept down a few hallways to do some snooping . . .

The English Alphabet

One of the first things I discovered is that English, as far as languages go, is not actually very old. It only began about 1,500 years ago (just a baby!). English began in a country called—you guessed it—England.

England is part of the islands known as Britain, which are just northwest of Europe. In the beginning, before English was even thought of, the local people in England and the surrounding countries of Scotland, Wales, and Ireland mostly spoke Celtic languages, which are completely different from English. But then, in about the fifth century AD, some noisy tribes from Germany paid England a visit. Quite a long visit, actually, and they brought their own language with them.

(At least they remembered to bring something!)

Some of these Germans were called Saxons, some were called Jutes and others Angles, which is where the word *English* eventually came from (think "angle-ish"). The German language they brought along is known as "Anglo-Saxon" or "Old English." But not only did they bring their own language, they remembered to pack their own alphabet as well. (Who would travel without one?) This alphabet was called runes and is what early Old English is written in. Have a look and see what you think:

ᚠ ᚢ ᚦ ᚠ ᚱ ᚲ ᚷ ᚹ ᚺ ᚾ ᛁ ᛥ
ᛃ ᛣ ᛦ ᛘ ᛏ ᛒ ᛗ ᛗ ᛚ ᛝ ᛉ ᛗ

So why don't we use runes to write English? Well, the Germans weren't the only ones to come and live in England. A whole lot of Christian monks from Europe and Ireland also turned up. They mainly spoke and wrote in Latin, using the Roman alphabet. After a while, naturally enough, they began to speak Anglo-Saxon/Old English too, but they wrote it in the Roman alphabet because it was easier for them than remembering all those runes. They did keep a few of the runic letters for a while, though, with lovely names like Eth, Thorn, Yogh, and Wynn. (Hmm, they sound a bit like some of the Word Snoop's relatives . . .)

So for a while Old English was written in a mixed-up Roman-and-runic sort of alphabet. When the Vikings turned up in the ninth and tenth centuries, the Old Norse they spoke used runes as well. But the monks, who did most of the writing, preferred to use the Roman alphabet to write Old English. Finally, William the Conqueror came across the sea from France in 1066 and conquered everyone. He and his fellow conquerors spoke and wrote in French, which also used the Roman alphabet. Those runes didn't stand a chance!

By the sixteenth century the English alphabet had more or less become the one we use today, with a few extra letters thrown in that the Romans didn't have, like J, V, and W. Admittedly Thorn (remember him?) was still hanging around, although by this time it looked like the letter Y. That's why if you ever get to see a book printed around that time, the word *the* is often written "ye." (Thorn stood for the sound *th*.) But as time passed, even Thorn finally withered away and we were left with the alphabet we use in English now.

Phew! That was a lot of snooping! I'm worn out, aren't you? Although I suppose it did take thousands of years to make our alphabet, so it was bound to be a long story. And probably it will go on changing as even more thousands of years pass. Just imagine what it might look like in the year AD 4000 . . .

Let's Change the Alphabet

It's a sad thing, but not everybody who writes in English loves the Roman alphabet. (Sob!)

The main complaint is that the Roman alphabet was really meant to write the sounds of Latin words, not English ones. In English, there are at least 40 different sounds, and yet the Roman alphabet (even with the extras thrown in, like J, V, and W) has only 26 letters. It's not surprising that all sorts of funny mixtures of letters have been used to create the sounds. But this has meant we've ended up with some pretty strange spelling rules (as I'm sure you would have noticed!).

Most of us think, *Oh well, that's the way it goes, better learn my spelling list (sigh) and be done with it* . . . But the Word Snoop has discovered that some people have more adventurous minds. The famous American thinker Benjamin Franklin, for one. He had ideas about all sorts of things, including the English language. Way back in 1779, he said we should change the alphabet to make spelling more sensible. He suggested kicking out C, J, Q, W, X, and Y, and replacing them with six new letters, including a special one for the sound *ng*.

Ten years later in 1789, another American, the dictionary maker Noah Webster, had a different idea. He thought we should put little lines or dots above the letters, like they have in French

and German, to show the different sounds. Then in the nineteenth century yet another American, the Mormon leader Brigham Young, suggested a whole new alphabet called Deseret that would make reading easier. Fifty years after that, the novelist Mark Twain, who wrote *The Adventures of Tom Sawyer,* added his complaints about our alphabet. He said, "It doesn't know how to spell, and can't be taught." (Tsk tsk, *bad* alphabet!)

Mark Twain thought the best idea would be to make the alphabet shorter. (Hooray!) But on the other side of the world, the Irish playwright George Bernard Shaw thought exactly the opposite. (Uh-oh.) He wanted to make the alphabet longer, with more letters for all the different sounds. Even though this might make learning to read and write seem harder at first, he was sure it would be worth it in the long run.

When Shaw died in 1950, he left instructions in his will for an "invent-a-new-sensible-alphabet" competition. A man called Kingsley Read won the prize of 500 pounds, or about 678 dollars, with his invention of the "Shavian alphabet." But only one book was ever published in this alphabet, a play called *Androcles and the Lion* by—you guessed it—George Bernard Shaw!

Invent your own Alphabet

All these people were trying to be useful (well, let's hope so) with their different alphabets. But what about inventing a whole new alphabet just for fun?

That's what J.R.R. Tolkien, the writer of *The Lord of the Rings,* did. He made up an Elvish alphabet, inspired by runes, for writing his own invented Elvish language. He'd been making up languages and alphabets since he was a schoolboy.

Here's an example of Tolkien's Elvish script:

ιϐ ᚛ᚂ ᚉ

The makers of *Star Trek* also invented a special alphabet for the fictional language Klingon. And in the *Star Wars* movies the language Aurebesh has its own script too. Here's what it looks like:

↓Ξϖ ▫△フフ ᴎⴷ△▫△ʋ

Can you guess what I've written? (Yes, my name does look rather strange . . .)

Now, if you were to make up your own alphabet, how would you go about it? You could start with another alphabet, as Tolkien did with runes, and play around with it and change it until you make it your own. Or you could invent something entirely new.

Try using the shapes of things you see around you. Remember the Phoenician alphabet? Those letters started off as pictures of things that the Phoenicians saw in their everyday life. For example, their word for ox was "aleph," so the letter we know as A was originally a picture of the head of an ox. B or "beth" was a house, C or "gimel" was a camel, and D or "daleth" was a door, and so on. Over time with lots of drawing, the picture became simpler and simpler, till you couldn't tell how it had started off.

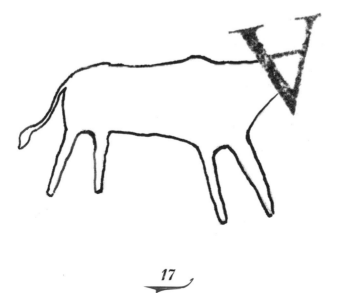

So for the letter for the sound *C*, for instance, you could draw a very simple picture, say, of a Cat. Or a Computer. Or a Cake. Or a Coconut. Or a . . . actually, I think I'll leave it to you!

Shorthand

Shorthand? What's that?

I can tell you one thing, you don't need a short hand to write it, but it sure takes a short time!

Have a look at this:

You might think this is just a lot of crazy squiggles that mean nothing at all. But actually it's not. Shorthand is not really an alphabet, but a special way of writing with symbols so that you can put down on paper very, very quickly what people are saying out loud. You can write with shorthand far more quickly than if you tried to write something down the ordinary way.

There are thousands of different shorthand systems, going right back to the ancient Greeks and Romans. The most famous is probably one called Pitman, invented by Englishman Sir Isaac Pitman in 1837. Usually journalists or court reporters use shorthand, so we can have a record of what people said. Nowadays there are computers with special keyboards so that you can type shorthand, which is even faster than writing it.

But shorthand has also been used as a way of writing secrets. Way back in the sixteenth century, Englishman Timothy Bright published a guide to his own shorthand, called *An Arte of Shorte, Swifte and Secrete Writing by Character.* (Sounds good for us Word Snoops, doesn't it?) And one of the most remarkable diary-keepers in all history, Englishman Samuel Pepys (pronounced *Peeps*), wrote 3,000 pages of his diary in such a particular shorthand that when he died no one could understand it. It took a lot of people over a hundred years to finally "translate" it back into English.

So if you knew shorthand, you could keep your own diary and write all sorts of secret messages with it. Like the squiggles on page 18—if you don't know shorthand, it could mean anything. I'll give you a hint, though. *The cat sat on* . . . Okay, okay, you guessed it!

Psst, Word Snoops! Remember how I mentioned a secret message at the start of this book? Well, here's the first part. But you'll have to crack the special code if you want to know what I'm saying. (Hint: Think about the alphabet, backward and forward . . .)

MLD GSZG BLF SZEV

Dear Snoops,

Have you ever noticed how strange English is?

For one thing, it has a lot of strange rules, especially for spelling. But what's worse, it has even more strange exceptions. An exception is something that breaks the rule. English has LOTS of very odd exceptions.

But why? That's exactly what I wondered, and I can tell you it took some pretty extreme snooping to find out.

Are you ready? You need to be sitting down in a nice, quiet, comfortable spot for this particular story . . .

Your comrade in espionage,

The Word Snoop

2.
Why
is English
so strange?

Silent Letters

$\mathcal{S}$hhh! It's time to talk about silent letters.

You know those pesky silent letters. They're the ones that creep sneakily into words at the beginning, middle, or end when you're not expecting them. Like the **k** in **k**nife, the **gh** in ni**gh**t, or the **b** in com**b**. (Aaagh! What are you doing there, silent letters! You frightened me!)

Have a look at this sentence:

The handsome ghost wriggled through the castle in half an hour.

Can you count how many silent letters there are? Eight? Or perhaps even more? Count them up for yourself. Come on, don't be silent . . .

English is not the only language with silent letters, but it has more than most. In fact, about 60 percent of words in English have a silent letter in them. This can be really hard when you're learning to spell, as you've probably realized already.

"K" NIFE

So why are those silent letters there? Well, it's all because of the mixed-up history of the English language. Remember how English began in about the fifth century AD when people from Germany settled in Celtic-speaking England? And then those Latin-speaking Christian monks turned up, followed in the ninth century by Norse-speaking Vikings? And then finally William the Conqueror appeared in the eleventh century with his French-speaking friends and conquered them all? (Why couldn't they all just stay quietly at home curled up sensibly by the fireside?)

Goodness. Celtic, German, Latin, Norse,

and now French speakers, each with their own language, alphabet, and system of spelling—it's a mystery how anybody understood each other! And actually, because William the Conqueror spoke French, for a while there French even became the official language of England. This is where quite a few of our silent letters crept in, from French words, where the **h** was not pronounced. For example, the silent **h** in **h**our comes from the French **h**eure (pronounced, um, "*er*"). I bet you can think of a few others like that. (Can't you? **H**onestly?)

Funnily enough, around this time people started putting letters into English words that weren't even French in the first place, to make them look more French. That's how the **u** was added to the original Latin word *color*—and it's still spelled "colour" like this in many English-speaking countries. (Though not in the U.S.!) Then other people thought it would be good if English looked more like Latin, so a **b**, for example, was dumped back into the word dou**b**t, even though it had been taken out because no one pronounced it that way anymore. And have you ever wondered about words like *psalm* and *rhubarb*? (Well, I have.) They came from ancient Greek words, which had ancient Greek letters, **psi** and **rho**. Oh, why couldn't they just leave poor old English alone!

So that's an explanation for some of our silent letters. Another important thing to know is that quite a few of today's silent letters have not always been so quiet. The word knight, for example, used to be pronounced in English with the **k** and the **gh** sounded out (*ke-nee-g-hht*), as were many of the silent **e**'s and **l**'s. And the silent **w** in words like **w**reck or **w**rite was originally there to show a funny sort of Old English **r** sound that was different from the ordinary **r**. But over time the way people spoke English changed, even though the spelling didn't.

And don't forget The Great Vowel Shift . . .

The what?

This strange happening started during the fifteenth century. What it meant was that gradually people began to change the way they said their vowels (a, e, i, o, u)—the sounds *shifted* to a different part of their mouth. Up until The Great Vowel Shift, a word like *met* was pronounced more like our word *mate,* and *goat* was pronounced more like *goot*. (Try saying them out loud and you'll see what I mean about your mouth.) Anyway, with these changes of pronunciation going on all over the place, letters in words appeared and disappeared as people wrote them down differently, and it all got even more confusing.

All right, you say, but this was hundreds of years ago. Why do we still use spellings based on how people *used* to speak?

Well, around the time of The Great Vowel Shift something truly extraordinary happened.

Are you ready . . . ?

The Invention
of Printing

What happened was something that truly CHANGED THE WORLD. It was a technological invention from Germany, which was just as amazing as the invention of the television or computers or the Internet.

This invention was—wait for it—the printing press! Now, while types of fixed printing, called block printing or stamping, had already been used in China for centuries, the mechanized printing press, with letters that could be moved around, was a brand-new invention that changed everything. Why? Well, believe it or not, until then all books in Europe had to be copied out by hand—usually by monks. It took ages just to make a single book, so there weren't many books around. People traveled for miles, even to different countries, just to read a book that was kept in a particular library.

But when Johannes Gutenberg invented the printing press in 1440, it meant that machines could print onto paper over and over again, and then the paper could be bound into books. By the end of the fifteenth century, there were thousands of books in print all over Europe. (Those lucky monks could heave a big sigh, put their pens down, and have a nice bath instead!)

In England, a printing press was set up in 1476 by a man called William Caxton. Although people spoke and spelled English differently all over the country, Caxton decided to print books in the type of English that people used in the biggest city—London. This is the kind of English that we now call Modern English, and it's basically what we speak and write—and spell—today.

Printing was very important for spelling, because the decision of how to spell words was left largely to the people running the printing press (just as before it had been left largely to the monks who copied the books out). The problem was that quite a lot of the printers were from Europe, and English was not their first language. So, even if they were good spellers, it was easy for them to make mistakes. (Just imagine us Word Snoops trying to decide how to spell something in Spanish, *por ejemplo*. I mean, for example!) This is thought to be the reason for the silent letter in the word **g**host, which was originally spelled without an **h**. Printers from Holland put the **h** in, because that's how they spelled it in their language.

But that was just one complication. Printers also affected spelling because they wanted printed pages to look nice and neat, with all the lines ending at the same place. (This is called justifying—you might have seen this option on

the computer.) In order to make printed lines longer or shorter, sometimes printers would decide to add an extra letter (an **e**, for example), or leave one off. This happened especially with what you might call unnecessary letters—such as the **k**, which used to be put at the ends of words like *music* (music**k**) and *logic* (logic**k**).

Now, once something's printed out, it can be hard to change. This was especially true back in the days when printing began, as one of the most popular books in print was the Bible. The printers felt very nervous about changing anything in the Bible, even if it didn't look quite right.

Even more importantly, there was still no

such thing as a standard dictionary with agreed "correct" spellings that the printers could look up to check a word as we would today. And let's face it, in the old days they didn't have quite the same idea of correct spelling as we do, anyway. The poet Geoffrey Chaucer, who wrote the famous *Canterbury Tales* in the fourteenth century, even seemed to have spelled a similar word two different ways in one sentence! See if you can spot it.

Nowher so besy a man as he . . . And yet
he semed bisier than he was.

But the arrival of printing meant that people became more interested in the idea of standard spelling and how a word should be written. They realized it would make life much easier for everyone if the spelling of a word was always the same.

This led to the beginnings of English dictionaries. The most famous and fascinating of the early English dictionaries was that of Dr. Samuel Johnson, published in 1755. Dr. Johnson loved the English language so much that he wanted to make sure its wonderful words would be looked after properly. He read thousands and thousands of books, letters, poems, and plays—and more—to find what he thought was the best spelling and meaning for a word.

So, next time you read a sentence, you'll realize you're seeing something very special. It may be that the word is spelled how it was pronounced hundreds of years ago, or according to a fashion, or just by mistake or confusion, or because somebody liked it like that. But all of those amazing spellings have been preserved, even frozen in the language, like fossils trapped in amber . . .

American Spelling

By the time Dr. Johnson was writing his dictionary, people from Britain had begun to roam around the world in ships and make settlements in lots of different countries. This was the beginning of something known as the British Empire. And just as William the Conqueror brought the French language with him to England when he conquered it, so these English people brought along English to all the different places they went. They spoke it, taught it, and published newspapers and books in it.

That's why English is spoken in so many different parts of the world—North America, Australia, Africa, and India, just to name a few. And in each place, naturally enough, a different kind of English developed, not just in accents or the way people pronounce words, but also in ways of making sentences and types of words—and yes, spelling.

Now, as you already know, not everybody likes English spelling, and there have been many calls to fix it up and get rid of things like silent letters. Probably the most successful act of spelling reform took place in the United States in the eighteenth century after the American Revolution, when America became independent from Britain. During this time, a man by  the name of Noah Webster (remember him from Chapter 1?) decided to write a dictionary of American English. He saw it as a big chance for a new country to improve all that pesky British spelling. Webster was particularly eager to get rid of what he described as "*silent letters; as a in bread. Thus bread, head, give, breast, built, meant, realm, friend, would be spelled, bred, hed, giv, brest, bilt, ment, relm, frend. Would this alteration produce any inconvenience, any embarrassment or expense? By no means.*"

Well, he didn't get everything he wanted (by no means!), but he did succeed in removing some silent letters from American spelling, like the **u** from colour (I mean, color), and the **gue** ending from words like dialo**gue** (I mean, dialog). But American English still has plenty of silent letters left behind that nobody seems able to chase away.

Over the centuries, thousands of dedicated, clever, and passionate people throughout the English-speaking world have argued sensibly and intelligently for spelling reform but, apart from Noah Webster, nobody's had much success. Although with e-mails and texting you can see there are some differences creeping in . . .

But I don't know, maybe we're all secretly fond of these silent letters. They're a bit like stray cats that wander into the house. After a while you just get used to seeing them there, and you might miss them if they went away. They remind you of all the people who have been speaking English for hundreds and hundreds of years before you.

Spelling Test

Geoffrey Chaucer was a wonderful, funny, imaginative poet who lived in England in the fourteenth century. Here's a quote from one of his poems. If you were his teacher marking it today, how many spelling mistakes would you spot? Try not to be too hard on him—remember there was no such thing as a dictionary then, let alone spellcheck . . .

But every thyng which schyneth as the gold,
Nis nat gold, as that I have herd it told

And what about this one?

And gladly wolde he lerne
and gladly teche.

Oh well, at least he got *and* right!

Plurals

It's not just spelling that makes English strange, though. What about plurals?

Plural means more than one. (I know, I know, you knew that already!) In English, when you want to make a word plural you just add an **s**. So a cat becomes cat**s**, sausage becomes sausage**s**, and—

But wait a minute. What about mouse? You can't say two mouse**s**. And what about sheep? There's no such thing as many sheep**s**. Or three woman**s**—and what about one knife and two kni**ves**? And one hero and two hero**es**. What's that all about?

You're right. It's not always just an **s**. (There they go again, those dastardly exceptions . . .)

The Anglo-Saxons (remember them?), who began the English language, had quite a few ways of making a plural. For some words they added **es**, but for others they added an **r** or an **en**, or sometimes both. This is why today we still say child and child**ren**, and ox and ox**en**. They also had plurals that changed the sound *inside* the word instead of at the end, like man and m**en**, foot and f**ee**t, tooth and t**ee**th. Then there were words in Anglo-Saxon that didn't change at all in the plural, like sheep and fish. And as for things like leaf and lea**ves**? Well, in Anglo-Saxon, an **f** at the end of a word sounded like **v** anyway, and over time somehow the **v** made its way into the plural spelling.

Now, I'm sure you haven't forgotten William-the-Conqueror-who-came-to-England-from-France-and-conquered-it-very-quickly. (Um, have you?) Anyway, as I was telling you, William and all his friends and relatives (there were lots of them) spoke French, and in French usually they just added an **s** to make a plural. This fine idea became popular in English as well, and is now the most common way to do it.

So, there are the Anglo-Saxon plurals and the French plurals, but there's yet another type of plural in English that you may have noticed—the Latin and Greek plurals. During the Renaissance (from the fourteenth to the sixteenth century), educated people felt that the ancient languages of Latin and Greek were really the best of all. So they started to throw Latin and Greek words into English—words like *crisis* or *radius*. But then, what if they wanted to mention more than one crisis or radius? Crisis**es** and radius**es** sounds terrible (especially if you happen to have a lisp). So instead they kept the Latin and Greek ways of making plurals for those sorts of words—cris**es** and rad**ii**.

That explains at least where some of these plurals come from. But, like the funny spellings, it doesn't explain why we don't just change it all to something easier. I mean, there are languages like Japanese and Chinese, spoken by millions and millions of people, that don't even have plurals and it doesn't bother anyone.

Well, I suppose in the end, language, like history, is made by human beings. And human beings are so hopelessly different and disorganized, they can never quite agree on anything. They're only human, after all. (Sigh.)

Still, maybe there's something special about

having these crazy plurals, and even crazier spellings. I sometimes think English is like a big old wall that people have been scribbling on for centuries. How sad it would be if someone came along and just sloshed a huge can of paint over the top of it, and everything disappeared and all we had left was a nice, clean wall . . .

Hooray for
Anglo-Saxon!

English is a language with a lot of different words—actually hundreds of thousands of them. If you ever look in a dictionary that tells you where a word originally comes from (this is called etymology), you will see that English words come from many different languages—French, Latin, Norse, Dutch, Greek, Hindi, Arabic, Yiddish, Japanese—and more.

But the first English words came from the German language called Anglo-Saxon—otherwise known as Old English. We owe a lot to those Anglo-Saxons. The days of the week, for example. Sunday, Monday, and Saturday are named after the sun, moon, and Saturn, but the other days take their names from Anglo-Saxon gods. So Tuesday is "Tiw's day" (god of battle); Wednesday is "Woden's day" (god of war); Thursday is "Thor's day" (god of thunder); and Friday is "Frigg's day" (goddess of love).

And even though there are now hundreds of thousands of other words in English, most of our common everyday words still come from Anglo-Saxon. Beautiful strong, short, simple words, like: *sun, moon, land, friend, hope, snow, shame, smile, groan, love, live, wife, house, child, man, fight.*

Don't be fooled, though. If we Word Snoops went back in time, we wouldn't be able to understand very much of what anyone was saying in those days. Anglo-Saxon was just too different to what we now speak, especially in how it sounded and was spelled. But if you're really interested, you can still learn Anglo-Saxon at college one day. (See you there!)

Hey, just for fun, have a look at the list on the opposite page and see if you can write a sentence that only uses Anglo-Saxon words. Here's a little Anglo-Saxon rhyme the Word Snoop just made up to give you an idea.

My brother eats cold cheese at night
And butter in the morning light.

(Mmm, yum!)

Some Anglo-Saxon words used in Modern English

a, and, at	good	noon
after	hill	rain
all	his, him, her	sea
bed	home	shirt
before	honey	shoe
brother	hope	sister
butter	house	smile
by	in, on, over	snow
cheese	land	sock
child	light	sorrow
cold	lightning	spring
day	live, love	star
drink	man	summer
earth	meat	sun
eat	midnight	the, then, there
egg	milk	thunder
father	moon	to
fear	morning	up
fight	mother	water
fire	my, me	why
friend	name	winter
go	night	with

Shakespeare and the Bible

Nowadays there are over a billion people in the world who speak English, but back in the sixteenth and seventeenth centuries in Britain there were only around five million. Yet from that small number came some of the greatest writers in the English language.

One was the playwright and actor William Shakespeare, who lived from 1564 to 1616. He wrote hundreds of poems and nearly forty plays, among them some of the most famous plays ever written—*Hamlet, Macbeth, Romeo and Juliet, Antony and Cleopatra, A Midsummer Night's Dream*—the list goes on. Even if you've never seen or read any of Shakespeare's plays, I bet you'll know some of the lines he wrote, because they are quoted everywhere—lines like "parting is such sweet sorrow"; "to be or not to be, that is the question"; "the game is up" and "good riddance!" (Ring any bells?)

Because Modern English was such a quickly

growing language when Shakespeare was alive, there are also hundreds of totally new words that were published for the first time in his plays. Words like *bedazzle, unearthly, madcap, bloodstained, watchdog*—and that's just a few of them. Some people think that Shakespeare may have invented these words himself—or it may be that he was just the first to write down words he heard people using around him. Whatever the case, Shakespeare's passion for English and his dazzling ability to turn words into rich, unforgettable stories and characters has made him the most loved writer in the history of the language. His work is read over and

over again, and has become part of all our lives, whether we know it or not.

The other writers from that early time who had a huge impact on how we speak and write English today were actually translators—people who change one language into another. How could they be so important? Well, it's because what they translated was the Bible.

The Bible, of course, was not originally in English, but in the ancient languages of Hebrew and Greek. As Christianity spread, the monks translated it into Latin, the language used in schools and universities. But then the idea began that it should be translated into English so that ordinary people (who didn't happen to know Hebrew or Greek or Latin) would be able to understand it.

Well, that probably sounds like a good plan to you, but many church leaders were against it. They thought that only educated people could truly understand the Bible, so it should stay in Latin or its original languages. In the sixteenth century, anyone who tried to translate the Bible into English could be arrested. The most gifted of these translators was a man called William

Tyndale. He was arrested, put in prison, and even executed in 1536. (Amazingly, he was so committed to his work he asked if he could have his Hebrew Bible, dictionary, and grammar book in prison so he could keep on translating!)

As time passed, luckily the church leaders changed their minds and decided it wasn't such a bad idea to have the Bible in English. So people were allowed to translate it without getting executed, and quite a few English Bibles were published. A few too many, really, as some of them were not very good. People were getting confused with so many different versions around. Finally, in 1611, during the reign of King James I, it was decided to get all the translations together and pick the best bits to make one extra-special official Bible that could be put in every church in the country. Known as the King James Bible, this became the regular Bible used by English speakers for at least the next 300 years.

The King James Bible is largely based on the translation of William Tyndale, who transformed the ancient foreign languages into dignified, astonishing, mysterious English. Like

Shakespeare, the King James Bible has been so loved, and read so many times over and over again, that thousands of its strange and beautiful phrases have become part of how we speak, think, and write. Here are just a few of the hundreds of expressions that have come to us in English via Hebrew and Greek from the King James Bible.

As old as the hills
By the skin of your teeth
A drop in the bucket
At your wits' end
From strength to strength
Let there be light
The salt of the earth
Bite the dust

Hello, dear Word Snoops. Did you figure out the secret message in the last chapter? Below is the next part, but of course you have to decipher the special code first. See how you do . . . (Hint: I wonder if any pesky silent letters have snuck into these words.)

FIGNAGLLGY
MALNALGELD TOK

Dear Snoops,

CANYOUREADTHISSENTENCE

Can you? There, I knew you could! It looks odd, though, doesn't it, without any punctuation. You know—periods, commas, question marks, quotation marks, that sort of thing.

But did you know that at one time there was no punctuation? Not only that, there were no spaces between words. And you didn't have to start your sentence with a capital, because ALL the letters were capitals.

SOHOWDIDANYONEMANAGETOREADANYTHING

You're about to find out . . .

Must dash—I see a comma coming, and an exclamation mark!

The Word Snoop

3.
Dots and
dashes,
interrobangs
and cat's
claws

Punctuation

When punctuation began, it was mainly to help people read out loud. Until a few hundred years ago, not many people were taught to read, so there was a lot more reading out loud by the few who could.

To help these out-loud readers in the ancient world, signs known as points were added to pages of writing. This is where the word *punctuation* comes from—the Latin word *punctus,* meaning "point." These points told readers when to pause, when to take a breath, and what to emphasize. They were a bit like all those notation marks in music that show you when to bang the piano really loudly, or when to play very, very slowly.

In Europe from the early centuries AD, these sorts of points were quite widely used, although not everybody used the same points for the same thing (here we go again!). But by the reign of King Charlemagne of France in the late eighth century, there was at least some agreement in Europe about a few of the signs, as well as things

55

like capital and lowercase letters, paragraphs, and spaces between words.

Then, when the printing press was invented in the fifteenth century, printers wanted some firmer guidelines about what to put where, so that everyone was doing the same thing. And now that more and more books were being printed, people started to think of punctuation as something that could help them make sense of what they were reading silently as well as out loud.

Since that time, all sorts of punctuation rules have been discovered, invented, and argued about, and many books have been written on the topic. You would have been taught some of the basic rules having to do with capital letters, periods, apostrophes, and commas at school. But even these rules have sometimes proved hard to pin down . . .

Punctuation: Signs & Symbols

Now you know *why* punctuation began—but how come we use those particular signs? And where did they get their names and shapes from? Well, after hours of careful snooping, here's what I managed to find out . . .

Comma, colon: period.

All three of these types of punctuation were given their Greek names by a friendly librarian named Aristophanes, who lived in Byzantium in the second century BC. They were marks on the page, each with a message to the reader.

Comma , meant a short pause. *Comma* is Greek for "cutting off."

Colon : meant a medium-sized pause. *Colon* is Greek for "limb" or a verse of a poem.

Period . meant a long pause — that is, a full stop. *Period* is Greek for "road going around."

Question mark ?

In the Middles Ages (from around the fifth to the sixteenth century), a squiggle above a period was sometimes used to show that the sentence was a question and that the person speaking should make their voice go up at the end. By the seventh century, it had turned into what we call a question mark. The curly shape may have come from drawing the letter Q—short for the Latin *Quaestio,* meaning "question."

Exclamation mark !

In the early days of punctuation, if you were reading out loud and you saw this sign above a period, you were supposed to make your voice sound amazed or surprised, much like we do today. Some people think the sign began as a squashed-up version of the ancient Greek word *IO* meaning "Oh gosh!" (or something like that), with the I on top and the O underneath. However it came about, it was well in use by the seventh century. At that time it was sometimes known as the "mark of admiration." (!)

Interrobang

More punctuation marks are being born all the time—just think of all the little signs you use when you're texting.

But have you ever seen this?

‽

It's an interrobang—a punctuation mark invented by Martin K. Speckter in 1962. It's especially for those moments when you want to use a question mark and an exclamation mark all at once. It could certainly be pretty useful for comic book writers!?!?!?

And have you ever heard of a question-comma or an exclamation-comma?

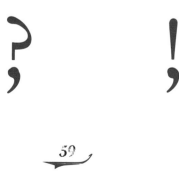

If you open up one of the books about Selby, the fabulous talking dog, chances are you'll spot one. These were featured in a book by the Australian author Duncan Ball, for those times when you want to use a question mark or an exclamation mark right in the middle of a sentence. Hey! why not use one yourself? next time you're writing a story.

Quotation marks " "

Quotation marks are used to show that someone is speaking. The kind we have in English today began to be widely used during the eighteenth century. Before that, readers simply understood from the way a sentence was written that someone was speaking, although sometimes the spoken words were underlined.

Apostrophe '

In English, the apostrophe is used for two things—to show where a letter or letters are missing (such as *don't,* for the missing **o** from "do n**ot**"); or to show who owns something (such as the *Word Snoop's umbrella*).

The word *apostrophe* is Greek. In ancient Greek drama, an apostrophe was when an actor turned away from the audience to address someone who wasn't there. (Perhaps they were at another play?) Anyway, the word came to be associated with the idea of standing in for something that was missing. So, for example, in Old English the letters **es** were used to show who owned something. Then the **e** started to be left out, and the apostrophe was put in to stand for that missing **e**.

Apostrophes are the punctuation mark that people seem to get most excited about—whether they love them or hate them. The Irish writer George Bernard Shaw didn't like apostrophes at all, and proudly wrote one of his most successful plays, *Pygmalion*, using as few as possible. But Lewis Carroll, the author of *Alice's Adventures in*

Wonderland, simply adored apostrophes and put in as many as he possibly could. For example, instead of writing *can't* (short for "ca**n** n**o**t"), he would write *ca'n't.* It must have taken him quite a while to write things down sometimes—"Sorry, I sha'n't come to play today. I ca'n't quite finish this letter . . ."

These days, you'll notice that sometimes when filling in a form you're asked to leave out the apostrophes altogether. This is because they can really confuse data entry systems. Lewis Carroll would be heartbroken!

Punctuation in Other Languages

Is it just me, or does this sentence look a little odd?

> *<<¿But how much is that doggie in the window?>> demanded Claudine.*

There's something about it . . . but what? Aha! It looks strange because it's using punctuation marks that come from languages other than English.

What? Even the punctuation is different?

That's right. Like anything to do with language, different groups of people have different ways of doing things. If you go snooping inside the font options on your computer, you'll discover several unusual kinds of punctuation from other languages that you may not have seen before. In Japanese, for example, the period is a tiny circle that is not filled in ∘ ; while in Hebrew it's a little black diamond ♦ . In Chinese, there's a special tear-shaped comma that you use when you are making a list ﹑ .

Have a look at the sentence on page 62 again, and let's see how sharp your snooping skills are. What do you notice? Yes, you got it! There are question marks at both the beginning and end of the question. Not only that, the question mark at the beginning ¿ is upside down. This is what you'd find if you looked at a book printed in Spanish. In an Arabic book, you might see the same question mark as in English, but pointing in the other direction ؟. In a Greek book, there's a different sign altogether, what we call a semicolon ; .

But what about those other funny signs? << >> They're the quotation marks. You'll also find them in languages such as Russian, French, and Finnish.

In some languages, they like their quotation marks so much they even give them nicknames. In Icelandic, they're called "goose feet"; in Turkish, "fingernail marks"; and in Hungarian, "cat's claws."

In English-speaking countries, printers and proofreaders who work with punctuation marks all the time (and get sick of saying the same words over and over again) have already thought of some good nicknames for them:

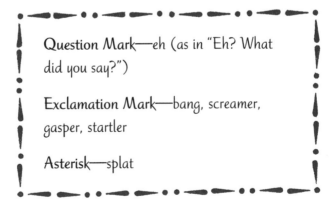

Question Mark—eh (as in "Eh? What did you say?")

Exclamation Mark—bang, screamer, gasper, startler

Asterisk—splat

Hmm, what nickname can you think of for a comma? Or a colon?

Punctuation:
Do we Need it?

The funny thing about punctuation is that it's actually not that hard to read without it, once you get used to it. Think of when you and a friend are texting—you hardly use any regular punctuation, but you can still understand each other. And in the Thai language, for example, there are rarely spaces between words and very few punctuation marks, but people keep reading anyway. After all, if you're not expecting to see something, you don't go looking for it.

Still, it's certainly true that punctuation can

sometimes help make the meaning of something clearer. The Word Snoop remembers the time she came home from school, and found this note left on the fridge door by her auntie:

> There won't be
> a single delicious
> ice-cream cake in
> here which will
> disappoint you.

Yum! I thought, picturing all those undisappointingly delicious ice-cream cakes inside. But when I opened the fridge door, I realized that my auntie actually meant:

> There won't be
> a single delicious
> ice-cream cake in
> here, which will
> disappoint you.

Hmmph! I should've written under the note,

I'm so disappointed I want to eat Auntie. Oops, I mean, *I'm so disappointed. I want to eat, Auntie!*

But luckily this kind of confusion happens far less often than you might think. And sometimes, when it does happen, it could be that the writer meant both things anyway—after all, writers just love double meanings and puns.

In the end, as with most things to do with language, writers will make different choices about punctuation because they think differently about sentences and words. It's part of the personality of their writing. William Shakespeare, for example, used almost eight times as many colons **:** in his seventeenth-century plays as we would nowadays, and in the eighteenth century, novelist Jane Austen used exclamation marks **!** far more often than her fellow novelist Daniel Defoe. In the nineteenth century, Swedish playwright Henrik Ibsen used four times as many dashes — as the Irish playwright George Bernard Shaw. Then in the twentieth century, dramatist John Galsworthy used four times as many semicolons **;** as playwright Eugene O'Neill.

So, as you can imagine, writers and editors,

students and teachers can spend a lot of time arguing about punctuation, because sometimes there's no "right" answer. The nineteenth-century Irish writer Oscar Wilde once reported that: "I was working on one of my poems all the morning, and took out a comma. In the afternoon I put it back again." (But what happened the day after that?)

Some writers HATE punctuation. The eighteenth-century American entrepreneur Timothy Dexter hated it so much that he included a separate page of periods and commas in a booklet he published. He said that readers who needed them were welcome to sprinkle them about wherever they wanted, like salt and pepper, but he wasn't going to put them in himself.

Then again, other writers LOVE punctuation. The seventeenth-century English writer Ben Jonson loved punctuation so much, he even added a colon between his first and last names— Ben:Jonson. (Nobody has ever figured out why exactly . . .) And when the noble German poet Goethe lay dying in 1832, he was seen to trace out words with his fingers, being very careful to include the correct punctuation marks.

It's hard to know whether Irishman James Joyce loved or hated punctuation. There is a whole chapter in his novel *Ulysses* with almost no punctuation at all, except right at the very end where he put—you guessed it—a period.

Whether you love or hate punctuation, maybe the best advice is just to enjoy it. It can even make you laugh. The Danish entertainer

Victor Borge did a very funny comedy sketch called "Phonetic Punctuation," where he made up a different wacky sound for each punctuation mark—for an em-dash, a colon, an exclamation mark, and so on. See if you can track down a recording of it (on the Internet, perhaps?).

I have to confess that I love punctuation. I love everything about it, even when people tell me I've got it all wrong! It would make me very sad if punctuation disappeared from our sentences. After all, punctuation has been around for more than a thousand years—the page would look undressed without it. Enjoy it, play with it, think about it, use it. It belongs to the language, and it belongs to you.

Happy punctuating!

! or ?

If you think about it, a single punctuation mark can carry a lot of meaning. Have you ever seen the episode of the TV sitcom *Seinfeld,* where one of the characters, Elaine, gets extremely upset with a friend who writes down a phone message and fails to add an exclamation mark at the end? And I bet you've sent an e-mail or text message with just a ! or a ? once in a while. Actually, back in the nineteenth century, long before texting was even thought of, the French writer Victor Hugo was worried about whether anyone would like his new novel, *Les Miserables.* He is said to have sent a message to his publisher containing only one thing, a question mark: ? The publisher sent him back a note with a single exclamation mark: !

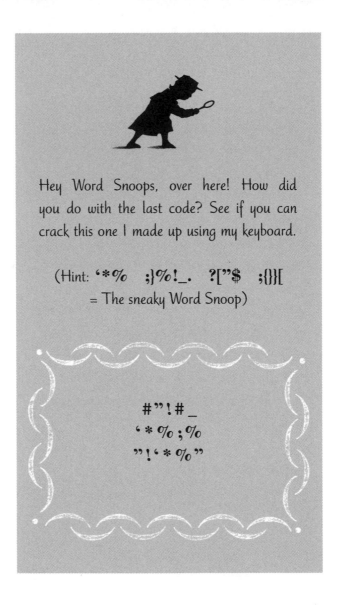

Hey Word Snoops, over here! How did you do with the last code? See if you can crack this one I made up using my keyboard.

(Hint: '*% ;}%!_. ?["$;{}[
= The sneaky Word Snoop)

#"!#_
'*%;%
"!'*%"

Dear Snoops,

I'm going to ask you all to close your eyes, take a deep breath, and relax. (Hey, don't go to sleep!) Now think back to when you were first learning to write your own name. How important and mysterious the letters seemed, each with its own special shape and sound.

Ever since writing began, people have been fascinated by the power of letters, and have played around with them in all sorts of unusual ways. Mixing them up, leaving them out, using them all at once—there are so many things you can do. The word for *letter* in ancient Greek is "gramma," and you'll see that word over and over again in this chapter with things like anagram, pangram and lipogram ...

What-a-gram???!!!

Watch and wait, my dear snoops, and you'll soon find out...

Yours snoopfully,

Doors went hop

4.
Letters,
letters,
letters

Anagrams

Have a look at these pairs of words:

LEMON/MELON
DANCE/CANED
ELVIS/LIVES

Look really hard at the letters. What do you notice about them? Well, in each pair, the two words are made up of exactly the same letters, they've just been arranged differently. This is called an anagram. The word comes from two ancient Greek words—*ana*, meaning "back" or "again," and *gramma*, meaning "letter." When you write the letters again in a different order, you get a whole new word.

Anagrams are often found in puzzle books or crosswords. But ancient Greek philosophers, like Plato and Pythagoras, thought that anagrams were more than just for fun—they believed anagrams revealed hidden meanings in words.

Later, mathematicians and scientists like

Galileo used anagrams as a code. They would put their discoveries into anagrams, so they could keep them a secret until they were ready to tell the world.

People have always enjoyed making anagrams out of their own names. An English mathematician, Augustus de Morgan, claimed to have made up about 800 anagrams from his name. King Louis XIII of France even had a Royal Anagrammatist, who would make anagrams of names on request. Twins sometimes have names that are anagrams of each other—like Tania and Anita, Claus and Lucas, or Ernie and Irene.

I wonder if you can make up an anagram of your own name? It doesn't have to be another name, it can be other words. An anagram of The Word Snoop, for example . . . Aha! Look back at the letter I wrote you at the start of this chapter and see if you can work it out . . .

Writers love anagrams. Samuel Butler wrote a novel about an imaginary country called Erewhon—can you figure out where it is? And what about the land of Tribnia that the Irish writer Jonathan Swift invented in his book

Gulliver's Travels? And in Lemony Snicket's *A Series of Unfortunate Events*, there's a very unpleasant character called Count Olaf, and another one named Al Funcoot, and another one called Dr. Flacutono, and another, Dr. O. Lucafont, and an even more unsavory medical couple, Dr. Tocuna and Nurse Flo . . .

Until recently, to work out an anagram you had to write all the letters down on a page in different orders, or use letter tiles and mix them up to find another word. It can be really hard to do. But now there are special computer programs that make up anagrams from any words you type in.

Still, it's fun to do it the old-fashioned way. See if you can work out the anagrams on the following page—or better still, think up some for yourselves!

Anagrams

1. Thorn, Shout, Seat, Stew (Hmm, which direction should we go?)
2. Listen (Where did all the noise go?)
3. Moon Starer (A student of the stars.)
4. Here come dots (Great way to send a message.)
5. The bear's in (And he's going to have a long, long nap . . .)

Pangrams

There's something special about the following sentence:

The five boxing wizards jump quickly.

Can you figure out what it is? Remember, it's all about *letters* . . .

Give up?

The answer is that it contains every letter of the alphabet—from A to Z. Have another look and check for yourself. Every single letter.

These kinds of sentences are called pangrams, which comes from two ancient Greek words—*pan,* meaning "all," and *gramma,* which you might remember means "letter." People have been writing pangrams for centuries, and not only with the English alphabet. There are pangrams in the Hebrew Bible, as well as in ancient Greek literature, such as Homer's *Odyssey.* And there's a pangram in Japanese that's more than a thousand years old—a poem called the *Iroha.*

Pangrams became most common after typewriters were invented in the late nineteenth century. This is because a pangram is a very quick way to make sure that all the keys on a keyboard are working. The most famous of all pangrams— *The quick brown fox jumps over a lazy dog*—was developed for this specific reason.

Pangrams are also a handy way of comparing all the letters in different fonts. Hmm, which do you prefer?

Amazingly few discotheques provide jukeboxes

or

Amazingly few discotheques provide jukeboxes

People are inventing new pangrams every day, just for the challenge. What's called a "perfect" pangram is one that contains only 26 letters in total, but they're very difficult to make up. Most pangrams contain many more letters than that.

A game you can play (and it's easier than inventing a pangram itself) is to write a story where each word begins with a different letter of the alphabet in order. To give you an idea, on the next page is one that the Word Snoop just made up.

A black **c**at **d**reamt **e**very **f**ourth **g**oose **h**unted **i**nvisible **j**ellyfish. **K**indly **l**et **m**any **n**ice **o**striches **p**ass **q**uickly. **R**ather **s**tupidly **t**he **u**mbrella **v**oted **w**hen **x**-raying **y**ellow **z**ebras.

Why not try to make up your own crazy pangrammatic story?

Lipograms

I bet you're wondering what a lipogram is. Um, a telegram with lips?

It might help to think of a pangram, which as we know is a sentence containing every letter of the alphabet. A lipogram is more or less the opposite of this. Instead of including *every* letter, you deliberately *leave out* a particular letter. The word comes from ancient Greek—*lipo*, meaning "lacking," and *gramma*, meaning—you guessed it—"letter."

Writing lipograms goes right back to at least the sixth century BC, when a Greek poet deliberately wrote verses where none of the words contained the letter S. This is called a lipogram on S. The question is—why did he do this?

NOBODY KNOWS.

In the eighteenth century, the German poet Gottlob Burmann apparently wrote 130 poems without the letter R—lipograms on R. He was even said to have avoided using any words with the letter R in his everyday speech! Try that— oops, I mean, attempt that!

Okay, but why?

DON'T ASK ME.

Of course, it's easier to write a lipogram on a letter that is not very common, like Z or Q. It's much much harder to write a lipogram on a letter like E, which is the most common letter in several languages, including English and French. Despite this, in 1939 Ernest Vincent Wright wrote a whole novel, *Gadsby*, without using a single E. He said that it was so difficult to write this book that he had to tie down the letter E on the keyboard of his typewriter to stop himself from using it. And following in his footsteps, in 1969 the French writer Georges Perec published a 300-page novel that also contained no E's. It's called *La Disparition*, which means "The Disappearance." (Where did that E go?)

But the question is—WHY? Why do writers

even want to do these strange things? What's wrong with just ordinary old sentences?

Well, I suppose it's because writers love language so much, they just want to play with it all day long to see what they can make it do, like making models out of clay. They are like experimenters in a laboratory. *Hmm*, they wonder, *what would happen if I did this? Or this? Where would this take me?*

Do you think you could make up a lipogram? (Or should I say, DO YOU ACTUALLY WANT TO?) Well, the Word Snoop has given it a whirl. Take a look at the sentences on the opposite page and see if you can work out what sort of lipograms they are . . .

Lipograms

1. For many days following, all boys and girls who had brought lollipops for lunch got a gold star.
2. I wonder why the huge octopus went to bed when the clock struck eleven?
3. Under his hat, the magician secretly kept a fluffy teddy bear.

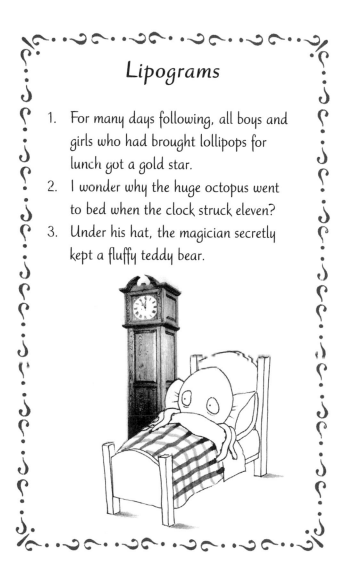

Acronyms

Acronyms
WDYS?
Acronyms
??
GAFOFY!
TFN
YW TTYL
NIICHI

Did you understand this conversation? Would it help if I told you it's written mainly in acronyms? Um, would it help if I told you what an acronym is?

The word comes from two ancient Greek words—*acro,* meaning "top," and *onoma,* meaning "name." An acronym is an abbreviation of a phrase or sentence, where you use only the beginning letter or letters of the words to say what you mean. So in the conversation above, WDYS? stands for **W**hat **D**id **Y**ou **S**ay? and

GAFOFY! stands for **G**o **A**nd **F**ind **O**ut **F**or **Y**ourself! Then it goes on: **T**hanks **F**or **N**othing. **Y**ou're **W**elcome. **T**alk **T**o **Y**ou **L**ater. **N**ot **I**f **I** **C**an **H**elp **I**t. (Gee, **N**VF . . . I mean, **N**ot **V**ery **F**riendly.)

These are the sorts of acronyms people use when texting a friend or talking in an Internet chat room. Internet slang languages, like LOL and Leet, are made up largely of acronyms. But acronyms have been around for thousands of years before the Internet was even invented.

Way back in the empire of ancient Rome, acronyms were used for inscriptions in stone. This was sensible, as it saved a lot of space and time and also stopped your hand from getting sore from too much carving. Instead of having to write **P**ia **F**idelis, meaning "pious and faithful," the stone carver only had to put the letters PF and everyone knew what it meant. (Let's hope so, anyway . . .) One of the most famous acronyms in all history, which was carved on many public monuments, is SPQR—**S**enatus**P**opulus**que**R**omanus, the "Senate and the People of Rome."

Another acronym you may have heard of

dates back to the second and third centuries AD. The early Christians used the very fishy word ICHTHUS to identify each other. It was an acronym of the Greek words **I**esous **Chris**tos **T**heou **Hu**ios **S**oter, meaning "Jesus Christ, Son of God, Savior." In this case, the acronym also spelled out the Greek word for "fish," which is why the fish is still a symbol used by some Christians today.

Acronyms are found in other religions too. In Islamic writing, you may see the acronym SAW written in brackets after the name of the Prophet Mohammed. It stands for the Arabic **S**alla **A**llahu alaihi **W**a Sallam, meaning "peace be upon him." And Catholic books and websites are full of Latin acronyms like AMDG (**A**d **M**ajorem **D**ei **G**loriam, "for the greater glory of God") and DV (**D**eo **V**olente, "God willing").

In the Jewish religion acronyms were particularly popular in the Middle Ages. Some people believed the Hebrew letters themselves had mystical meanings, which made acronyms very special, and they were used in prayers and blessings and things like that. Important rabbis were even known by acronyms of their names—for example, the eleventh-century Jewish leader **R**abbi **I**saac **B**en **A**sher was also called RIBA.

But the real explosion in acronyms happened in the twentieth century. It was actually during World War Two (I mean, WWII) in the 1940s that the word *acronym* first started being widely used—and you can see why! The army had lots and lots of acronyms—not only for all the divisions and ranks of officers, but also for things like the COMAMPHIBFORSOPAC (**Com**mander, **Amphib**ious **For**ce, **So**uth **Pac**ific). Phew! And let's hope no one you know of was ever KDPOW (**K**illed or **D**ied while a **P**risoner **Of W**ar).

After WWII, acronyms had become so fashionable it seemed almost every new organization had one—UNESCO, NATO, UNICEF, and many others. It was the same in the field of science and technology. New discoveries were being made all the time, and some words were so long and strange that it made sense to use acronyms. Let's face it, **DNA** is much easier to say and remember than **D**eoxyribo**n**ucleic **A**cid.

Not everybody liked all these acronyms, though. The English writer George Orwell certainly didn't. In his novel set in the future called *1984* (well, that was the future way back then!), he invented a kind of language called Newspeak, where the government used acronyms and abbreviations on purpose to hide what was really going on. Orwell had noticed that Nazi and Communist governments did this with some not-very-pleasant organizations like the SS (**S**chutz **S**taffel, "protective squad") and the

NKGB (**N**arodnyi **K**omissariat **G**osudarstven-noi **B**ezopasnosti, "People's Commissariat of State Security"). He thought once a government starts using a lot of acronyms, it was definitely BN (**B**ad **N**ews).

But sometimes acronyms are JFF (**J**ust **F**or **F**un). The novelist P. G. Wodehouse created a lovely, silly character called Bertie Wooster, who scattered ridiculous acronyms throughout his conversations, such as "I put my F in my H" ("I put my **F**ace in my **H**ands") or "In my humble O" ("In my humble **O**pinion"). These are more like the acronyms used in text messages, e-mails and chat rooms. In fact, IMHO is one of the most commonly used!

Sometimes, groups of people who use a lot of acronyms in their work forget that other people have no idea what they're talking about. Every profession seems to have its own set of peculiar acronyms. But here's a tip from the Word Snoop—don't despair if you come across a really unusual acronym. Go to the Internet and look up an acronym-finder website, and it will explain unknown acronyms for you.

LLL (Latin, Latin, Latin)

Funnily enough, a few of the really common acronyms we use in everyday life don't even come from English but from Latin, the language of the ancient Romans. This is because Latin was used in schools and universities as a common language in Europe right up until at least the fifteenth century. So AM and PM, which you know mean "morning" and "afternoon," actually stand for the Latin words **A**nte **M**eridiem and **P**ost **M**eridiem, meaning "before midday" and "after midday."

And PS, those two letters you put at the end of an e-mail or a letter when you want to add something extra, stands for **P**ost **S**criptum, which means "after writing." Then there's i.e. or **i**d **e**st, which means "that is"; and e.g. or **e**xempli **g**ratia, which means "for example." And, of course, our old friend etc.—**et c**etera, which means "and the rest of them."

Now, what about AD and BC? Well, AD dates back to the sixth century AD, and is short for **A**nno **D**omini, "in the year of the Lord." The "Lord" is the Christian leader Jesus Christ, who was determined to have been born in AD 1. It wasn't until several hundred years later that people felt they wanted an acronym for all those centuries before AD. By then English was more popular than Latin, so BC simply stands for **B**efore **C**hrist. (No translation needed!)

Well-mannered acronyms

AD and BC come from the Christian religion, but they've been used in many countries and cultures over the years, including non-Christian ones. More and more, though, you'll see BCE and CE instead, which stand for **B**efore **C**ommon **E**ra and **C**ommon **E**ra. Some people like it better than AD and BC, because it doesn't sound so religious. It's still referring to the birth of Jesus Christ, of course, just not saying it OUT LOUD (shhh!).

Another foreign language acronym that's also rather polite is RSVP, which stands for the French **R**espondez **S**'il **V**ous **P**lait, meaning "please answer." This was adopted in English as a delicate way of reminding people that it's good manners to answer the invitation, OR ELSE!

Dot dot dot

When acronyms were less common, it was usual to write them in capital letters with periods after each initial—like U.S.A. (**U**nited **S**tates of **A**merica) or C.A.T. (**C**omputed **A**xial **T**omography) scan. Nowadays, while the periods are more often left out, the capitals still remain—USA, CAT—to show it was once an acronym.

Sometimes a word will become so common that both the periods and the capitals disappear, and hardly anyone remembers that it was ever an acronym. So L.A.S.E.R. (**L**ight **A**mplification by **S**timulated **E**mission of **R**adiation) became LASER and is now just plain old laser. That's what you call a really successful acronym. (Well done!)

And finally the backronym . . .

Sometimes acronyms have been worked out backward to fit a word that already exists. They're called backronyms. People do this for lots of different reasons:

* to make you laugh, e.g., PICNIC—
  Problem **I**n **C**hair **N**ot **I**n **C**omputer

* to tell you what to do, e.g., DEAR—**D**rop
  Everything **A**nd **R**ead

* to give something complicated a simple
  name, so that it's easier to identify
  or sell, e.g., the computer language
  BASIC—**B**eginners **A**ll-purpose **S**ymbolic
  Instruction **C**ode

* to help you remember something
  important, e.g., the Olympic gold-medalist
  Cathy Freeman used the backronym FLAG
  to help her win races—**F**ly **L**eg-speed
  Attack **G**o!

* as a kind of brain teaser, where the words
  that make up the acronym actually explain
  what it means, e.g., SPAM—**S**tupid
  Pointless **A**nnoying **M**essages

And then there are the Word Snoop's
favorite backronyms, the ones that form a

secret code. During WWII, soldiers who were posted overseas would write backronyms, using the names of countries, on the backs of letters they sent home. Now, if the person receiving it didn't know it was a backronym, they would just frown and say, "How very peculiar!" But if they understood . . . aha!

Don't get too excited, though; they were mainly love letters. So ITALY on the back of an envelope meant "**I T**rust **A**nd **L**ove **Y**ou" and HOLLAND meant "**H**ope **O**ur **L**ove **L**asts **A**nd **N**ever **D**ies." (Ahh.)

Hmm. What do you think MALAYA stood for? Well, it could be:

My **A**untie **L**ucy **A**te **Y**our **A**pple

or

My **A**rdent **L**ips **A**wait **Y**our **A**rrival

I bet you could make up some amazing backronyms out of the names of countries yourself. Go on, give it a try—it doesn't have to be a love letter (that's a relief!). Any sort of secret message will do. Here are a few the Word Snoop just made up:

JAPAN (**J**elly **A**nd **P**ies **A**re **N**ice)
SYRIA (**S**end **Y**our **R**ed **I**guana **A**way)

Why don't you try with TONGA or CHILE? Or, for a real challenge, what about UZBEKISTAN!

Me again, Word Snoops! My guess is you're getting very good at cracking codes by now. See how you do with this one. (Hint: Think about what a lipogram is.)

REAE AN ASTARLY COES

Answers

ANAGRAMS

1. North. South, East, West
2. Silent
3. Astronomer
4. The Morse Code
5. Hibernates

LIPOGRAMS

1. Lipogram on E
2. Lipogram on A
3. Lipogram on O

Dear Snoops,

Is anyone watching? Or listening?
Are you sure? Okay then, so we can talk.

Can you speak Greek? It's a handy language for
us Word Snoops. You've probably noticed a few
Greek words in this book already. This is because
in the old days at universities people often learned
ancient Greek so they could read all the wonderful
books the ancient Greeks wrote—comedy, tragedy,
history, mathematics, philosophy—you name it.
People's minds were so full of Greek words, they
kept slipping them into English.

Maybe one day you'll be able to learn ancient
Greek too. In the meantime, remember the Greek
alphabet is different from ours. When you change
a Greek word to English, you have to
transliterate it—change from one alphabet to
another. It's a bit tricky, but useful for writing
secret messages...

Your friend,
θε υορδ σνοοπ . . .

5.

Is that another Greek word?

Palindromes

Palindromes are words or sentences that are spelled the same backward or forward. The word *palindrome* comes from two ancient Greek words—*palin,* meaning "back again," and *dromos,* meaning "running"—so it's a word that runs forward and then back again. Look closely at the words EYE, NOON, and RADAR. It doesn't matter at which end you start writing the word, it's spelled the same. This means they are palindromes.

The ancient Greeks and Romans enjoyed making palindromes, especially for inscriptions on public monuments, but lots of languages have them. In English, the longest common word that is a palindrome is REDIVIDER. But in Finnish, the word for a soapstone seller, believe it or not, is a palindrome—SAIPPUAKIVIKAUPPIAS. (Now that's an unusual occupation—soapstone, anyone?)

Palindromes can be found in names like Hannah, Otto, Pip, or Aviva, or places like Glenelg (where they even have an annual palindrome festival!). And then there's always ABBA, the

Swedish pop group. But a whole sentence can be a palindrome. Have a look at the ones below. Ignore the punctuation and the gaps, just look at the letters.

Go, dog!
Was it a cat I saw?
Don't nod.
Do geese see God?

WAS IT A CAT I SAW

Believe it or not, in 1969 the French writer Georges Perec wrote a palindromic story that was 500 words long! The whole story reads the same backward as forward. It would have been very difficult to do, and it was a very strange piece of writing. In fact, some people who read it didn't realize it was a palindrome and thought he had gone mad . . .

The comedian Weird Al Yankovic wrote a song of palindromes about singer Bob Dylan. Try singing this:

Madam, I'm Adam
Too hot to hoot
No lemons, no melon
Too bad I hid a boot

Wow! (Hey, that's a palindrome too.)

WOWWOW

I wonder if you can make up your own palin-drome song? First, you need a supply of words. To get you started, try to figure out the palin-dromes on the opposite page, but I'm sure you can think of lots more yourself.

Palindromes

1. Another name for *father*
2. The sound of popcorn cooking
3. More red
4. A kind of canoe
5. If you're in the Scouts, you'll try to do a good one of these every day
6. The sound a horn makes
7. Another word for peek

Mnemonics

Many Venomous Earwigs Munch Jelly Sausages
Underneath Nests.

I think this sentence is trying to tell me something—and not just about venomous earwigs. This is actually a mnemonic (pronounced *nem-on-ik*). A mnemonic is the word for tricks we can play with our minds to help us remember things. Like the order of the planets in the solar system . . .

Mercury Venus Earth Mars Jupiter
Saturn Uranus Neptune

Do you see? The beginning letters of each word in that first sentence stand for the beginning letters of the planets in the order they appear in the sky. For some reason, it's easier to remember a silly sentence than the names of the planets themselves.

The word *mnemonic* comes from one of the Titans in ancient Greek mythology. Her name was Mnemosyne (*Nem-oss-in-ee*) and she represented memory. In the ancient world, memory was especially important when there weren't many books and not many people learned to read. People used to memorize pages and pages of the books everyone wanted to hear, like *The Odyssey* or the Bible, and hundreds of types of mnemonics were developed to help them do this. Nowadays we would find it incredible that people could remember that much, but of course back then they didn't have a choice. It wasn't until the fifteenth century, after the printing press was invented, that the need for such amazing acts of memory fell away.

But not totally! There are still things we need to remember. When the Word Snoop was at school, she learned the Great Lakes from west to east across Michigan with the sentence: Sam's Horse Must Eat Oats—*Superior, Huron, Michigan, Erie, Ontario*. (You'd be surprised how often this information comes in handy . . .)

There are many different types of mnemonics. For example, to remember the difference between spelling desert and dessert, you can say "the sweet one has two sugars." (Two S's, get it?)

And what about the rhyme to remember the number of days in each month ("Thirty days has September . . ." and so on). That's a mnemonic too. And have you seen the episode of *The Simpsons* when Bart and Lisa help Marge to study for a big exam by putting all the facts she needs to remember to the tune of a song? I bet your teacher or your parents might know some mnemonic tricks like this. (Go on, ask them.)

You can have lots of fun with mnemonics. In music, children often learn a mnemonic for the order the notes come on the staff: *Every Good Boy Deserves Fruit* (E G B D F). But look what other people have made up to remember the same thing: *Empty Garbage Before Dad Freaks; Elephants Go Bouncing Down Freeways; Evil Godzilla Buys Dog Food.*

Here's one the Word Snoop just invented—can you guess what it stands for?

Remarkable Children Understand Challenging Books

(Hint: Think of the five largest countries.)

Why don't you make up a mnemonic of your

own? Come on, Word Snoops—have fun, and improve your memory at the same time!

Oxymorons

Oxymoron. (Don't you mean foxymoron? No, I mean oxymoron!) It's one of those words you don't forget once you've heard it. But what on earth does it mean?

Like lots of unusual words in English, it comes from the language of the ancient Greeks—*oxys*, which means "sharp," and *moros*, which means "silly" or "dull." It's used to describe expressions that contain two opposite ideas—in other words, something that is "sharply dull."

Hmm, maybe some examples would help. Has anyone ever said to you, "that's *old news*"? This is an oxymoron because it's contradicting itself—news can't be old, because it's *new*. And then there's that song by Simon and Garfunkel, "The *Sound* of *Silence*." How can silence have sound? So that's an oxymoron too. And so is the cartoon character Charlie Brown's favorite line—"*Good grief!*"

Writers have been using oxymorons for thousands of years, all over the world, in many languages and cultures. The ancient Chinese philosopher Lao-Tzu said, "To *lead* the people, walk *behind* them," and the English playwright William Shakespeare wrote, "I do *believe* her, though I know she *lies*." The nineteenth-century French novelist Victor Hugo spoke of "the *pleasure* of being *sad*," and in the twentieth century, the American poet T. S. Eliot described the "*pleasant whining* of a mandolin." Well, they all sound like very interesting gentlemen . . .

Because oxymorons have a way of grabbing your attention, you will often find them in advertising. You know, things like *genuine imitation* or *seriously funny*. Movie titles also use oxymorons to make you look twice—think of *Back to the Future, Eyes Wide Shut*, or *True Lies*.

And then there are those people who like to use oxymorons as a form of humor. Like your teacher might say, "I've got some *lovely homework* for you today." (Ha ha.) Or, "I want a *compulsory volunteer* to clean up the playground." (Hilarious.) Well, you could always answer back, "Excuse me, you are *clearly confused*."

I wonder why oxymorons are so appealing? Perhaps it's because an oxymoron is really a kind of paradox—something that appears to be true and false at the same time. The world can sometimes seem so large and strange, and many human experiences just don't make sense. As the great poet Walt Whitman wrote, "Do I contradict myself? Very well, then, I contradict myself. (I am large—I contain multitudes.)" (Gosh!)

Maybe an oxymoron is a way for a writer to express those mixed-up feelings—and hopefully for a reader to try to understand them. So next time you're writing a story or a poem or a report on something, why don't you try putting in an oxymoron or two?

In the meantime, try spotting the oxymorons on the next page in the story that the Word Snoop made up about a little dog.

A tragicomedy of a lost dog

A gigantic Chihuahua was hurrying slowly
along the soft, stony road. He came to
a low tower of delicious rotten turnips.
Daintily he wolfed them down. But
then his tummy felt as light as a bag of
cement, so he decided to have a long nap.
Instantly his owner finally arrived.

"Fluffy!" whispered his owner in a loud
voice, fondly pulling the dog's hairless fur.
"You darling little monster. I think I might
have definitely missed you."

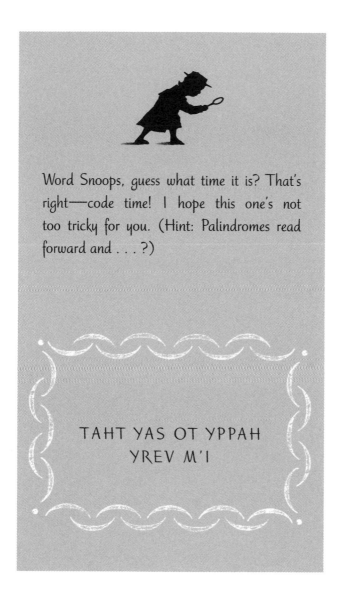

Word Snoops, guess what time it is? That's right—code time! I hope this one's not too tricky for you. (Hint: Palindromes read forward and . . . ?)

TAHT YAS OT YPPAH
YREV M'I

Answers

PALINDROMES

1. Dad
2. Pop
3. Redder
4. Kayak
5. Deed
6. Toot
7. Peep

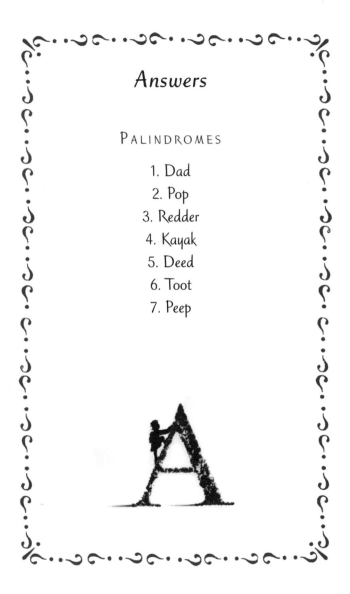

Dear Snoops,

It's time for some FUN!

YAY!!!

Okay, calm down for a moment. We're going to play some games, but you'll still need to have your brains switched on.

You see, you can play games with bats and balls and toys and a hundred other things, but you can also have a great time playing with words. You can play around with the sounds, or the meanings, or both at once—and anything else you can find.

Come on, let's play!

Your ludic friend,

The Ord-way Noop-say

P.S. What do you think the Word Snoop's favorite game is? Yep, you guessed it— I Spy!

6.

Who likes playing games?

Pig Latin

Have you ever wanted to speak a secret language? Here's an easy one to learn. It's called Pig Latin.

Now, Latin is the language that the ancient Romans used to speak, and you know what pigs are. (Hint: They go *oink, oink*!) Can pigs really speak Latin? Well, no, actually. Pig Latin has got nothing to do with Latin or pigs. It's just a funny kind of language-game children and adults have been playing for years. Like rhyming slang, it may have started as a kind of thieves' language, a way of disguising what you were saying to confuse anyone who might have been listening.

Even though nobody really knows who started it, or why it's called Pig Latin, we do know that it's been around since at least the 1920s—in the playground, in movies, in songs and in stories. The famous old movie star Ginger Rogers sang a song in Pig Latin in the movie *Gold Diggers of 1933*. And if you ever get a chance, listen to the wonderful folk singer Lead Belly singing

"The Pig Latin Song," which he recorded way back in the 1940s. Do some snooping and see if you can still find a recording of it online.

When the Word Snoop was at school, all the children in the playground spoke Pig Latin. Maybe your teacher knows it, or your parents, or your grandparents. But it's not just old folks. Even Krusty the Clown on *The Simpsons* has been known to speak a bit of Pig Latin!

Here's how it works. It's pretty easy, once you get the hang of it. Take away the first letter of the word you want to say, and put it at the end of that word. So for the word DOG, for example, take away the D and put it at the end, so you've got OG-D. Then you follow it by the two letters AY. That's it! So DOG in Pig Latin becomes OG-DAY. Can you work out what CAT would be? Think about it. That's right—AT-CAY!

See! Easy-ay! Oh! That reminds me. There's just one more rule. If a word begins with a vowel (a, e, i, o, u), then you just put AY on the end of the word, without taking the first letter away. So the word EASY, as you see, just becomes EASY-AY. And if a word begins with something like a CH or a TH or a SH, like SHAKE THAT

CHOP, you take the whole sound, not just the first letter—AKE-SHAY AT-THAY OP-CHAY! (Not that hard!)

At first it might seem difficult to remember, but once you get a bit of practice you'll be able to say whole sentences quite easily. Somebody has even translated the Bible into Pig Latin. Wow! I mean, OW-WAY!

Pig Latin is a game for the English language, but lots of other places in the world have similar secret languages that children love to play around with, although some of them are a lot more complicated than Pig Latin. In Argentina there's something called *Jeringozo*, in France there's *Verlan*, and in Japan, *Ba-bi-bu-be-bo*. Maybe you or someone you know speaks a language that has its own kind of Pig Latin?

Can you work out what this message in Pig Latin means?

> ODAY-TAY IS-AY Y-MAY
>
> IRTHDAY-BAY.
>
> AN-CAY OU-YAY OME-CAY
>
> O-TAY Y-MAY ARTY-PAY?
>
> MM-HAY. AYBE-MAY. I'LL-AY INK-THAY
>
> ABOUT-AY IT-AY.

(Pssst! If you get stuck, check out the Answers page at the end of the chapter.)

The Rebus

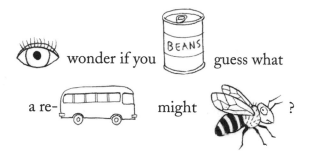

wonder if you guess what a re- might ?

This strange-looking sentence is called a rebus, which is a kind of picture puzzle. *Rebus* is Latin for "by things," and in a rebus sentence you use pictures of things in place of words or parts of words. The person reading the rebus has to use the pictures to work out what it means.

Sometimes in a rebus you simply use a picture instead of a word, so a picture of a cat is used for the word *cat*. But in a true rebus, the pictures don't mean what they *look* like, they mean what they *sound* like. So in the rebus at the top of the page, the picture of an eye doesn't mean "eye," it means "I," which is another word that sounds the same. And the picture of the can doesn't mean a can of beans, but the word *can,* meaning "able to." See if you can work out the whole sentence now.

This way of communicating words through pictures has been around for thousands of years, going back as far as some of the ancient Egyptian hieroglyphs. Rebuses are handy if you have a lot of people who can't read, so they were popular in the Middle Ages, especially for things like coats of arms. Sometimes these were jokes—for example, the coat of arms of a family named *Islip* has a picture of an eye, and then a man falling out of a tree. (I-slip, get it?) Hmm, could you make up a rebus like this for your surname?

Over the years, rebuses have appeared in lots of unusual places. For example, the sixteenth-century artist Leonardo da Vinci, who painted the famous *Mona Lisa,* was fascinated by rebuses and sometimes put them in his paintings. In 1661 a Norwegian poet, Nils Thomasson, published a long wedding poem of rebuses, together with a set of instructions on how to make them up. Later, in the eighteenth century, rebuses were used as a kind of code by people in France wanting to spread secret messages. And during the American Revolution, a rebus was a popular way to write a thank-you letter or even a love letter. Lewis Carroll, the English writer of *Alice's*

Adventures in Wonderland, also liked to send rebus letters, usually to children to make them laugh.

If you look around nowadays, rebuses are everywhere—on the Internet, in advertisements, on T-shirts, even on television game shows. Often they use letters and numbers instead of pictures, like you do in text messages. So the number 4 will mean "for," or the letter *R* stands for the word "are."

Why do people love rebuses so much? Well,

the Austrian psychoanalyst Dr. Sigmund Freud believed it was a very natural way to think. He said that when you have a strange dream, you should look at it as a kind of rebus, where words and pictures and symbols and sounds are all mixed up together. So, if you dream about a big hand holding a key, maybe you're really dreaming about your hankie. (Then again, it could just be someone trying to unlock the door . . .)

Anyway, whatever the reason, rebuses are fun! Why don't you make up some yourself? You could try single words to begin with, then see if you can do a whole sentence. Here's one to get you started. Can you work it out?

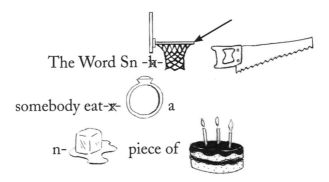

Rhyming Slang

You may never have heard of rhyming slang, but I'm sure you can use your *down the drain* and work it out. (Hint: What rhymes with "drain"?)

The rule of rhyming slang is that instead of a word, you say another word or name or phrase that rhymes with it. So instead of saying money, you say *bread and honey,* instead of mate, you say *china plate,* instead of a pie with tomato sauce, you say *a dog's eye with dead moss.* (Erk, no thanks!)

And this is my china plate.

It's like a code. That's how rhyming slang is supposed to have started, actually, over a hundred years ago amongst people known as Cockneys from the East End of London in England. They are said to have invented it to keep things secret. This was particularly useful if you were a *tea leaf* on the run from the police, and you didn't want to spend time in *ginger ale*. (Hint: What rhymes with "leaf" and "ale"?)

Rhyming slang quickly became popular in many other places in the world, and it's still used today, with new rhymes being made up all the time. Have a *Captain Cook* at the dialog on the opposite page and see if you can work out what Mr. and Mrs. Rimer are really saying to each other.

First to finish is the *chicken dinner*!

Mr. and Mrs. Rimer at breakfast

Mr. R: Good morning, treacle tart. How are you?

Mrs. R: I had a terrible sleep, turtle dove. I was banging my head on the weeping willow all night.

Mr. R: Tsk, tsk, that's no good. I'll put a bit of Uncle Fred in the roller coaster for you.

Mrs. R: Hmm, thanks. Any lady in silk left in the Brooklyn Bridge?

(There's a noise outside)

Mr. R: Excuse me a moment, my dear, I just heard a Highland fling at the door.

(He goes out and returns with a set of keys.)

Mrs. R: Who was that? One of the local dustbin lids?

Mr. R: No, it was someone who found my macaroni and cheese on the field of wheat.

Mrs. R: Well, isn't that rubber ducky!

Mr. R: Yes, so finish up your molten toffee and I'll take you out for a nice spin in the jam jar.

Hey there, clever Word Snoops. Another day,
another code . . . See if you can work out the
next part to my message. (Hint: Think rebus.)

URA
SECRET ←
SECRET
SECRET
SECRET
SECRET
SECRET

Answers

PIG LATIN
Today is my birthday. Can you come
to my party?
Hmm. Maybe. I'll think about it.

THE REBUS
I wonder if you can guess what a rebus
might be?

The Word Snoop saw somebody eating
a nice piece of cake.

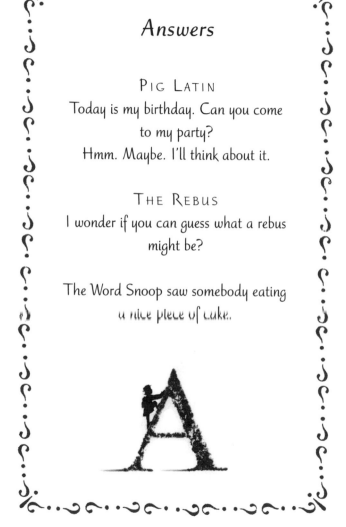

Dear Snoops,

Tra-la-la!

Do you like to sing? Words begin as sounds, just like music and singing. Writing only comes later. In this part of the book, I'm going to tell you about some of the weird and lovely things I've discovered in my travels that have to do with the **sounds** of words.

Writers love how words sound, sometimes even more than what they mean. Plays, poems, novels—so much writing is full of **puns, homophones, onomatopoeia,** as well as other playful things like **anagrams, acronyms, oxymorons, tautologies, lipograms, palindromes** . . .

Gosh! Is that the time? I'd better be going. I've got some more snooping to do . . .

Abyssinia! (I'll be seeing ya, get it?)

The Whirred's Noop

7.
Say
that
again!

Puns

Knock knock!
Who's there?
Lena.
Lena who?
Lean a little closer and I'll tell you.

Do you know what a pun is? If you laughed at this joke, then maybe you do! A pun is a way of using a word (or words) so that it has more than one meaning. So in this joke, *Lena* is a girl's name, but it also sounds the same as "lean a." HA HA HA HA! (You can stop laughing now.)

Puns make us laugh because they take our brains by surprise, like seeing a funny picture when you're not expecting it. Most knock-knock jokes use puns. Nobody knows who invented the knock-knock joke, but they seem to have begun in the 1950s with school children in South Africa. Now there are millions of them out there. Plenty of other types of jokes use puns as well. See if you can spot the double meanings in the ones on the next page.

Shops and businesses often use puns in their

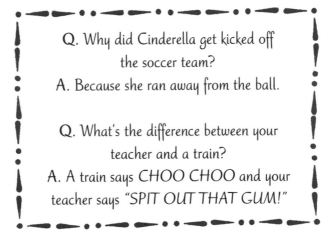

Q. Why did Cinderella get kicked off
the soccer team?
A. Because she ran away from the ball.

Q. What's the difference between your
teacher and a train?
A. A train says CHOO CHOO and your
teacher says "SPIT OUT THAT GUM!"

names. A shop that specializes in reading glasses could be called *Special-Eyes,* for example, or a shop that washes your dog could be *The Laundro-Mutt* (like Laundromat—get it?). Have you seen some others?

Sometimes writers use puns to make you laugh and think at the same time—the Irish playwright Oscar Wilde was an expert at these sorts of witty puns. Even the title of his most famous play is a pun, *The Importance of Being Earnest*—Ernest is a man's name and *earnest* means "to be honest."

But puns don't have to be funny. Another

Irishman, Samuel Beckett, loved puns so much he even wrote in one of his very serious novels, "In the beginning was the pun." (So then what happened?) And in the play *Romeo and Juliet* by

Bark!

William Shakespeare, when one of the characters is dying after being stabbed in a fight he says: "Ask for me tomorrow, and you shall find me a *grave* man." (Because *grave* means "serious" as well as—stop laughing, it's not funny!)

Be warned, puns won't always make you popular. The most common response to a good pun is a big GROAN . . . As Lewis Carroll, who was rather fond of puns himself, said:

> *The Good and Great must ever shun*
> *That reckless and abandoned one*
> *Who stoops to perpetrate a pun.*

Anyway, don't worry about that. Everyone knows that children come up with all the best puns. I bet you can think of plenty.

Have a pun time!

Homophones

Puns depend for the most part on something called homophones. A homophone is the name people use when you have two or more words that sound exactly the same but have different meanings, and are sometimes spelled differently too. It comes from (you guessed it!) two ancient Greek words—*homos*, meaning "same," and *phonos*, meaning "sound."

All languages have homophones. It's pretty natural, given all the things and ideas in the world, and how most languages use a limited number of sounds. Chinese is thought to have the most homophones of all, but English has quite a few

too. You can find lists of them on the Internet, and in libraries there are whole books of them.

Some homophones in English are thought to have come about because of that rather drastic event I told you of before, The Great Vowel Shift (gulp!), when people started changing the way they said their vowels. So, for example, the words *meet* and *meat* weren't homophones originally, as they were pronounced differently (the word *meat* used to sound more like "mate"). In the same way, whether something is a homophone or not depends on how you pronounce English. For example, the words *offal* and *awful* are homophones for some English speakers, but not others. (How offally confusing!)

Yes, well, homophones can be confusing. That's why when you're reading you really have to be grateful for all those silent letters and strange spellings that English is full of. (I knew there had to be something good about all that!) In a book or a story, you'll never mistake a *knight* for a *night*, or a *symbol* for a *cymbal*, or "I would like a *two*, *too*" for "I would like a *tutu*."

Unless it was a particularly strange story . . .

Mondegreens

Oh my darling, oh my darling,
Oh my darling, lemon pie!
You are lost and gone forever
Dreadful sorry, lemon pie.

Gee, what a sad song! Poor person, to lose their lemon pie. Could someone get me a hankie?

Hang on a minute. What kind of person sings such a sad song about losing their darling lemon pie? Well, nobody, actually. This is just how some people hear the words of the song "Oh My Darling, Clementine." Sometimes, especially when everyone sings together, the words aren't very clear, and "Clementine" can sound a bit like *lemon pie*. Say it aloud for yourself a few times, and you'll see what I mean.

This is something called a mondegreen. It's what happens when we hear words without reading them and our brains have to work out what we think is being said or, more often, sung. The writer Sylvia Wright invented the word in 1954 from something she misheard as a child in a poem her mother used to recite:

"They have slain the Earl of Murray,
And *they laid him on the green*."

which she heard as:

"They have slain the Earl of Murray,
And *the Lady Mondegreen*."

Poor Lady Mondegreen!

Mondegreens happen because of all the homophones and oronyms in English, which are words and groups of words that sound similar but

are spelled differently and mean different things. Mondegreens are mistakes, but they're fun and interesting mistakes. They show us how we listen—first for sounds, then words, then meaning. And they can also reveal things about the mind of the person who does the mishearing . . .

There are lots of mondegreens out there. Do you know the book *Olive the Other Reindeer* by Vivian Walsh and J.otto Seibold? The title comes from a mondegreen in the Christmas carol "Rudolph the Red-Nosed Reindeer," where "all of the other reindeer" has been misheard by children for years as *Olive, the other reindeer.* Now Olive is famous!

Probably the funniest mondegreens are from pop songs, like *there's a bathroom on the right* for "there's a bad moon on the rise," or *baking carrot biscuits* for "taking care of business." Sometimes people don't realize for years (or ever) that the words could be anything else . . .

I bet you can think of some words in songs or poems or prayers that you used to sing but found out later weren't the original lyrics. In the meantime, see if you can work out what the mondegreens on the next page are.

Mondegreens

1. José, can you sing?
2. Sleep in heavenly peas
3. The ants are my friends, they're blowing in the wind
4. Knock, knock, knocking on Kevin's door

Onomatopoeia

WOW! That's a hard word! *Ono-mato-pee-a.* Hmm. Actually, you probably use onomatopoeia every day. Like when you *crunch* on a very juicy apple and *slurp* as you lick all the juice from your face, or listen for the *brrring* of the bell when school's over (at last!).

The word *onomatopoeia* comes from ancient Greek. *Onoma* means "name," and *poeia* means "making." Onomatopoeia is when you use a name or word that makes the sound of something, or at least suggests it somehow. For an easy example, remember the fights in *Batman*? *POW! WHAM! SMASH!* That's onomatopoeia. Comic-book writers love it. In fact, there's even an evil comic-book character called Onomatopoeia, who gets his name by imitating sounds, like the dripping of a faucet or a gun going off. (Keep away from him!)

The words for animal sounds often use onomatopoeia, like *moo* for a cow, or *quack* for a duck. But the funny thing is, even though animals sound much the same all over the world, people who speak different languages make up

different words for the sounds animals make. So, for example, in English a pig goes *oink oink*, but in Chinese it's *hu lu*, in Croatian it's *rok rok*, and in Portuguese *croinh croinh*. An Indonesian dog goes *gong gong*, a Russian dog *gav gav*, and an Albanian dog *hum hum*. Try that out next time you sing "Old Macdonald Had a Farm!"

And it's not just the animals. If you're in Japan and someone cracks a joke, make sure you don't say "ha ha ha," because in Japan it's *hu hu hu*. Or if you're in Poland and you feel a big sneeze coming on, don't say "aah-choo!" when you sneeze, say *apsik!* And luckily when the Word Snoop was in Bulgaria last summer and someone stepped on her toe, she remembered just in time to cry out *"Ox!"*

Poets are especially fond of onomatopoeia, where the sounds and the meanings of words go together. What do you think the writer Edgar Allan Poe, famous for his scary stories and poems, was talking about here?

"How they *tinkle, tinkle, tinkle,*
In the icy air of night!"

(No, not daggers—think *ding dong* . . .)

In *The Giants and the Joneses* by Julia Donaldson, the giants speak a language that the author made up herself called "Groilish," with words like *heehuckerly* for "funny" and *glishglursh* for "splash." And in Roald Dahl's *The BFG* (yes, that's an acronym), there are words like *frobscottle* and *trogglehumpers*. What do you think they could mean?

You could make up some words like this. It could be giants talking, or it could just be based on something ordinary, like a ride on a tram or a train or a bus. To give you an idea, ask your grandparents or a VERY old teacher if they can sing you "The Trolley Song," made famous by the singer Judy Garland. It's got *clangs* and *dings* and *zings* and *chugs* and *bumps* and *buzzes* as well.

In the meantime, see if you can work out what the onomatopoeic words on the opposite page could be.

Onomatopoeia

1. A game you play with two bats and a lightweight ball across a table. (Don't hit too hard!)

2. The sound a snake makes. (Leave the room very quickly when you hear this sound.)

3. A bird you might find in a wooden clock. (Not exactly alive.)

4. When you talk in a very low voice. (As you always should. Ha ha! Or should I say hu hu?)

Tongue Twisters

Say the following sentence as fast as you can three times.

Betty Botter bought a bit of bitter butter.

Not bad. Now try:

Bobby Blue blows blue bubbles.

Or even just:

Mixed biscuits, mixed biscuits.

Did you notice what happens to the words? For most people, the words all start to tumble together and trip over each other. This is something called a tongue twister. Tongue twisters are fun sentences or phrases that are hard for your tongue to say, especially if you try to say them quickly.

Your tongue is a very important part of your mouth for making sounds of words. Tongue twisters are tricky because they use words that repeat similar sounds. Look at all the **b**'s and **it**'s in ***Betty Botter bought a bit of bitter butter***. And the **i** and **s** and **x** sounds in *mixed biscuits*. When similar sounds come close together over and over again, our tongue and our brain get mixed up.

In the olden days, tongue twisters were thought to be magical, like spells. Nowadays they are mainly just for fun. But they can be used for special reasons as well. Actors often warm up their voices with tongue twisters. And sometimes speech therapists will use tongue twisters to help someone who finds it hard to make particular sounds.

Two very old and well-known tongue twisters you might have heard of in English are:

Peter Piper picked a peck of pickled peppers.

and

She sells seashells by the seashore.

But all languages in the world have tongue twisters. *Kelapa kepala,* for example, is a tongue twister in Indonesian (it means something like "coconut head"). Maybe you know a tongue twister in another language?

Some poets have written amazing tongue twisters into their works. The English poet Gerard Manley Hopkins wrote some totally tongue-twistery poems that are difficult to recite, but at the same time are very strange and beautiful. Try saying this out loud:

I caught this morning morning's minion,
kingdom of daylight's dauphin, dapple-dawn-
drawn falcon

Or this line by the poet Sylvia Plath:

Black lake, black boat, two black, cut-paper people

Those are more serious tongue twisters. But if you feel like something to make you laugh out loud, see if you can find a recording of "Tongue Twisters" sung by the comedian Danny Kaye. Try singing the two verses on the next page.

Moses supposes his toeses are roses
But Moses supposes erroneously
For Moses he knowses his toeses aren't roses
As Moses supposes his toeses to be

Theda thought Thora was thumping her thimble
But Thomas thought Thora was thumping her drum
Said Theda if Thora's not thumping her thimble
I think that she surely is thumping her thumb

Danny Kaye had such a twisty tongue that in a song called "Tchaikovsky and other Russians" he managed to name 54 Russian composers with very difficult names in 38 seconds!

The best fun, though, is making up your own tongue twisters. You could try using the sounds in your name. For example, if your name is Mike, you could say something like:

Mike makes mad mud cakes.

Or the Word Snoop could say:

Why would the weird Word Snoop loop the hoop?

Why indeed?

Go on, get your tongues twisting!

Portmanteau Words

Mmm, I'm feeling hungry. Look at the time—it's about half past ten in the morning. Too late for breakfast, too early for lunch . . . I know, I'll have *brunch*!

Brunch is a portmanteau word. That's a word that is a blend or mixture of two different words—like *breakfast* and *lunch*. These sorts of words can be handy. For example, if you look outside the window and see all the smoke and fog mixed up together, what have you got? You guessed it—*smog*!

The name *portmanteau* was given to these sorts of words by the writer Lewis Carroll over a hundred years ago in his wonderful book *Through the Looking-Glass and What Alice Found There*. In those days *portmanteau* was a French word for a special kind of suitcase that had two separate compartments inside it. Alice asks one of the characters, Humpty Dumpty (yep, the famous egg himself), to explain what these lines from a crazy-sounding poem "The Jabberwocky" mean.

> *'Twas brillig and the slithy toves*
> *Did gyre and gimble in the wabe.*
> *All mimsy were the borogroves*
> *And the mome raths outgrabe.*

Humpty Dumpty begins his explanation: "Well, 'slithy' means 'lithe and slimy.' Lithe is the same as 'active.' You see it's like a portmanteau—there are two meanings packed up into one word." The word *chortle* was actually invented in this poem—a portmanteau word made up of chuckle and snort. (Now that really makes me *snuckle*!)

A portmanteau word is different from a *compound* word—that's when you have a word made up of two whole and different words put together, like *loudmouth, football,* or *blackboard.* With a portmanteau word, the two words blend into each other and usually each loses a bit of itself to fit into the other one. So while Labrador-poodle would be a compound word, *Labradoodle* is a portmanteau word. And have you ever heard of a *tigon*? (Or do I mean a *liger*?) If you are a Pokémon fan you will have noticed many of the monster species have portmanteau names, like *Turtwig* (turtle and twig) or *Torchic* (torch and chick). Do you know any others?

Some portmanteau words have been around so long we forget that's how they came about. *Electrocute,* for example, comes from electrify and execute; *ginormous* is a mix of gigantic and enormous. Then there are the more recently

snurtle

invented words like *podcast*, made up of iPod and broadcast, or things like *docudrama* and *mock-umentary*. And what about *romcom*? Now that's an abbreviated-rhyming-portmanteau-word! (Have you figured it out? That's right, "romantic comedy.")

Why not make up your own portmanteau words? You can use any sorts of words. For instance, an animal that's a mixture of a rhi-noceros and a kangaroo could be a *rhinaroo*. Or what time of day do you think it would be if I said to you, "Good *aftorning*!" And how about a hamburger with lots of legs—a *burgerpillar*. (I think I might try drawing some of these . . .)

On the next page are some portmanteau words children have made up—can you work out what they are?

Pormanteau Words

1. A troop of brave **commangos** ran up the hill.
2. I want to go inside, but I'm just too **nervited**!
3. I'm not asleep, I'm just **threaming**.
4. Do you know how to play the **pianpet**?

Well, Word Snoops, there's not much of my secret message to go. But you'll need to decipher this code if you want to read the full sentence. (Hint: Did you read the chapter on mondegreens?)

FOOL LEAK WALLY

FIE DAND

Answers

MONDEGREENS

1. Oh, say can you see?
2. Sleep in heavenly peace
3. The answer, my friends, is blowing in the wind
4. Knock, knock, knocking on heaven's door

ONOMATOPOEIA

1. Ping-Pong   2. Hiss
3. Cuckoo   4. Murmur

PORTMANTEAU WORDS

1. Fighting mangos—a cross between "commando" and "mangos"
2. When you feel "nervous" and "excited"
3. A cross between "dreaming" and "thinking"
4. An instrument that is half "piano," half "trumpet"

Dear Snoops,

Words are sneaky. Sneaky, tricky, and hidden. (A bit like the Word Snoop.) You never quite know what they're saying to you, or what they really mean, or what traps they're hiding. You have to listen very carefully sometimes, and speak and write even more carefully.

But don't be afraid!

If you fall down a hole into a terrible deep darkness, I'll pull you out.

Right after I pull myself out, actually . . .

Read on,

Yours ever watchfully, AAAAAAAAAHH!!!

The Word Snoop

8.

Hmm,
I wonder
what you're
really
saying . . .

Euphemisms

I wonder, do you think Alfred really liked the present that Aunt Martha sent him? Have a good look at what he's written. What can you discover about the sweater? That it's too big, that it's a color nobody else would like . . . Why doesn't he just say so? Well, it can be hard to say that sort of thing directly. At times like this, we often use something called euphemisms.

A euphemism is the name given to the ways we find to say things that people don't really want to hear or that make them feel uncomfortable. The word *euphemism* comes from the ancient Greek words *eu,* meaning "good," and *pheme,* meaning "something spoken."

One of the earliest euphemisms was the name the Greeks gave to some of their goddesses called the Furies. The Furies were not very pleasant—they had hair made of snakes and drove people to their deaths. (Urgh!) Understandably, they made the Greeks feel a bit nervous, so instead of calling them "the Furies," they called them by the euphemism "the Kindly Ones"! Maybe they thought they might forget to be furious and become kind instead. (It was worth a try . . .)

Most euphemisms are used for things people find embarrassing to say out loud. For example, in restaurants the toilets are often called *restrooms*—and let's face it, you're not going to lie down and have a little sleep in there, are you? (Are you?)

Funnily enough, the word *toilet* itself was originally a euphemism. It's from a French word *toile,* a piece of cloth you used to put around your neck while washing, or on your dressing table. It started to be used as a euphemism for the . . . you know, the . . . Anyway, now we think even the word *toilet* is not quite polite!

Once you start listening or looking, you'll find euphemisms everywhere. It might not be a particular expression, but a way of saying something indirectly, like Alfred's letter. It's pretty handy when you have to break some bad news. Like:

"Hey, have you ever thought of getting a pet mouse?"

(Translation: Your guinea pig just escaped from its cage and ran off down the street.)

Or: *"Luckily, you won't have to leave room for dessert tonight."*

(Translation: I just finished all the chocolate mousse and now there's none left.)

Don't Mention It

Death, which nobody likes to think about, probably has the most euphemisms of any word. Some of them are: *passed away, no longer with us, sleeping with the fishes, permanently out of print*—on and on they go.

The British comedy team Monty Python did a very funny sketch you may have seen about a man who brings a dead parrot back to the pet shop where he bought it. The man tries to tell the pet-shop owner that the parrot is dead, but the owner pretends not to get the message. The man uses every euphemism he can think of. He says the bird is:

bereft of life
gone to meet his maker
fallen off the twig
pushing up daisies
passed on
kicked the bucket
joined the choir invisible, etc. etc.

Finally he shouts out in exasperation: "This is an *EX-PARROT*!"

Euphemisms for death are often used out of kindness, because the truth can be so painful. Read the scene on the next page from Charles Dickens's wonderful novel *David Copperfield.* David is away at boarding school and is being told that his mother has died.

"When you came away from home at the end of the vacation," said Mrs. Creakle, after a pause, "were they all well?" After another pause, "Was your mama well?"

I trembled without distinctly knowing why, and still looked at her earnestly, making no attempt to answer.

"Because," said she, "I grieve to tell you that I hear this morning that your mama is very ill."

A mist rose between Mrs. Creakle and me, and her figure seemed to move in it for an instant. Then I felt the burning tears run down my face, and it was steady again.

"She is very dangerously ill," she added.

I knew all now.

"She is dead."

There was no need to tell me so. I had already broken out into a desolate cry, and felt an orphan in the wide world.

It's definitely kinder at times to use euphemisms than to say something straight out. This is probably why teachers are such experts at euphemisms, especially in school reports. Parents who think their child is adorable might get upset if they hear that she mucks around a lot and never stops talking, so instead the teacher will write on her report card that she is *always coming up with fascinating ideas to liven up the classroom* and has *truly astonishing vocal cords.*

Hmm, what do you think the teacher was trying to say on these pupils' report cards?

Gretchen has a remarkable feel for color.

Octavio is very thorough and never rushes his tasks.

Lupin always takes a great interest in the work of his classmates.

(Translations: Gretchen regularly spills paint everywhere; Octavio is always the last to pack up at the end of the day; Lupin copies other people's answers.)

Doublespeak

There's another sort of euphemism sometimes known as doublespeak. It comes about not from kindness or embarrassment, but from the need to hide the truth, or make something that's not very appealing sound better.

This happens a lot when people are buying and selling. Look at advertisements in the newspaper or on the Internet. *Pre-loved* means anything secondhand. A *historic property* could mean a house that's so old it's falling to pieces. And let's face it, *nice leafy garden* sounds better than "previous owner planted huge patch of lettuces."

Doublespeak is particularly useful when something has gone wrong and nobody wants to admit it. For example, if the school cafeteria was robbed overnight and all the food was stolen, the principal might stand up in assembly and say, "Unfortunately the cafeteria will not be opening today owing to an *unexpected lack of supplies.*" After all, nobody wants to admit to leaving the door to the cafeteria unlocked, do they?

Charles Dickens wrote about the dark side

of this sort of euphemism in his novel *Little Dorrit*. In *Little Dorrit*, there's a terrible place called the "Circumlocution Office," where no one ever says what they really mean. *Circumlocutio* is Latin for "roundabout speech"—that is, saying something with so many words that it's difficult to tell what's actually being said. This kind of euphemism was made fun of in the 1980s British television series *Yes Minister,* which was about a government office where people used a lot of words to make sure nobody could understand them. For example, if a character said *The matter is under consideration,* what they really meant was "we've lost the file." (If they said *The matter is under* active *consideration,* it meant they were desperately trying to find the file!)

Have a look at the statements on the next page issued by a modern-day Circumlocution Office. Can you figure out what on earth they're trying to tell you? (Hint: They are well-known proverbs.)

Doublespeak

1. A piece of round red or green tree fruit that is commonly used in pies served with ice cream if ingested once every twenty-four hours will ensure that the medical practitioner remains at a distance.

2. Refrain from enumerating the offspring of your hens prior to their exit from the eggshell.

Clichés

I was **scared to death**. I knew my turn was coming. I sat pretending to be **cool as a cucumber** while I waited for the bell to ring. It **seemed to take forever** and I lost track of time. Then the **next thing I knew** it was lunchtime. **Saved by the bell!** I ran outside, **free as a bird**, without a care in the world . . .

Can you guess why the Word Snoop has put some of the words in the little story above in bold? Well, it's because each of those expressions is something called a cliché (pronounced *clee-shay*). Clichés are phrases that you have heard and read so many times, they don't really carry much meaning or excitement anymore.

The word *cliché* goes back to France in the eighteenth century, when printing was done by making metal plates with the letters placed on them. A particular kind of fixed metal plate, called a *stereotype,* was invented as a quick, cheap way to print something over and over again, instead of making up a new plate each time. *Cliché* (meaning "clicked") was a word for the sound the plate made in the press, and was often used for the name of the plate itself.

But although it was a cheaper and quicker method of printing, the print quality of these clichés and stereotypes was not as good as setting up new printing blocks each time. So the words came to be used for characters or expressions in writing that are weak copies, rather than being fresh and original.

Clichés are everywhere—in newspapers, books, television, radio, and songs. Why do we use so many? Well, I suppose the whole reason a cliché comes about is because the first time the expression is used, it seems to describe something really well—that's why it gets repeated so often and becomes a cliché. When people are in the grip of their deepest emotions, they often use clichés to sum up how they're feeling: "I'm totally shattered" or "This is too good to be true."

If you look at the Bible or plays by William

Shakespeare, they seem to be full of clichés, with phrases like "by the skin of your teeth" or "there's method in his madness." But these weren't clichés to begin with. They were expressions that people liked, and so kept on saying. The problem is, once you say something too many times, it can lose the meaning it had in the first place.

There are writers, though, who use clichés on purpose. The nineteenth-century French novelist Gustave Flaubert made characters think or speak in clichés because he wanted to show the reader that's how some people actually think and speak. Other writers play around with clichés and create something called an *anti-cliché*. The Big Bad Wolf is a bit of a cliché—okay, so why not write a story about the Big Good Wolf? That's

an anti-cliché. But then if everyone does it, the Big Good Wolf becomes a cliché too. Then what do you do? (An anti-anti-cliché?)

It's very difficult to avoid clichés completely. The problem with clichés is that they're *so* familiar that you don't even notice you're using them. You can get computer programs now that will look for clichés in your writing and highlight them. What you see might *shock you to the bone!* Oops ... um ... I mean, *shock your socks off* ... I mean, *shock you out of your mind.* Oh dear. How about *may cause disturbance to some viewers* ... ? Gee, this is harder than it looks!

Take a look at the little story on page 180 and see if you can rewrite it without the clichés. Which version is more enjoyable to read? And to write?

Tautology

Watch out for the *frozen ice!*

You may not know it, but this sentence is something called a tautology. It comes from two Greek words—*tautos,* which means "same," and *logos,* which means "word."

A tautology is when you repeat something in a sentence when you don't have to, because the information is already there.

In that first sentence, ice is always frozen (otherwise it wouldn't be ice), so there is no need to describe it as frozen. You can just say: "Watch out for the ice!" In the same way, if you say that someone is a *famous celebrity,* it's a tautology because a celebrity has to be famous, otherwise they're not a celebrity. (Well, that's the idea, anyway . . .)

Tautologies are far more often said out loud than written down. Your brain takes a bit more time when it's writing, and usually you realize the problem and fix it up. But when you're talking, words come out very rapidly, before you can think too much. People who have to speak a lot in public, like sports commentators and politicians, come up with the most tautologies. Like the ones on the next page.

"If we don't succeed, then we will fail." (Aha!)

"He's on the final lap, which is the last one." (Good to know.)

"The plan was to rob the banks illegally." (The things people do . . .)

"The person who wrote this book must be some kind of author." (Some kind of what?)

The Australian playwright Alexander Buzo collected these sorts of funny tautologics and published whole books of them. Tautologies like this are sometimes known as "Yogiisms," after the baseball player and sports commentator Yogi Berra. He's the one credited with the phrase "It ain't *over* till it's *over*." (Yeah, but, like, when is it over?)

There are some expressions or names we use that are actually tautologies but we don't realize it. This happens particularly if other languages are involved. The name of the country East Timor, for example, means "East East" because *timur* in Indonesian means "east." In the supermarket you might see Chai Tea for sale—in Hindi *chai* already means "tea." (Would you like a nice cup of tea tea?) The same thing can happen with acronyms, when words are shortened to their initials and we forget what the initials stood for in the first place. ATM machine is a tautology, because ATM stands for "Automatic Teller Machine." (Automatic Teller Machine machine?) And why is PIN number a tautology?

As far back as the sixteenth century, grammar books have said that tautologies are a kind of mistake. But actually, they're not always mistakes—sometimes writers may be using them deliberately on purpose (ha!), to make you pay more attention, or make you laugh or think. William Shakespeare, who many people think was the greatest writer the world has ever known, wrote this famous tautology in his play *Julius Caesar*—"this was the *most unkindest* cut *of all.*"

You'll see plenty of deliberate tautologies in

advertising, where they want to make sure you really get the message. Here are just a few the Word Snoop has spotted on her travels:

Free gift
Open every day, including Sunday
Bargain Basement Downstairs

(Gosh, thanks for telling me, I might have headed upstairs . . .)

On the next page is a telephone conversation between two friends that contains quite a few tautologies. I wonder if you can spot them . . .

"Have you heard? The Word Snoop has written her own autobiography."

"Is that really true? What an unexpected surprise!"

"Oh well, I suppose she's just following her natural instinct."

"Can you repeat that again? I didn't hear the inaudible part."

"Sorry, must go. Look at the time! It's already five p.m. in the afternoon."

"Okay, bye. See you when I see you!"

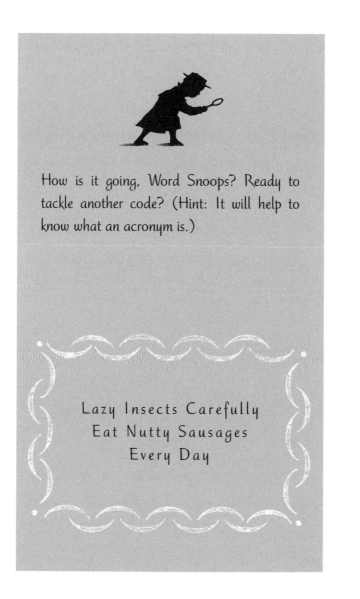

How is it going, Word Snoops? Ready to tackle another code? (Hint: It will help to know what an acronym is.)

Lazy Insects Carefully
Eat Nutty Sausages
Every Day

Answers

DOUBLESPEAK

1. An apple a day keeps the doctor away.
2. Don't count your chickens before they hatch.

Dear Snoops,

Names are special things. Most people are pretty attached to their names. And some people have more than one name, for quite a few different reasons . . .

Sometimes, a person's name even turns into another word altogether, and becomes famous—more famous than the person ever was!

What am I talking about?
Turn the page to find out . . .

Yours in name (and in deed),

The Word Snoop

9.
Is that
a real
person?

Nicknames

A nickname is a special name that your friends and family call you. It shows that they know you well, and usually that they like you too. When the Word Snoop was at school, her nickname was *Urk*. (Erk!)

The word *nickname* comes from the Middle English word *eke*, meaning "to increase," added to the word *name* (so to "add to a name"). Over time, the words "an *eke* name" said over and over again turned into "a nickname."

Nicknames are actually how a lot of surnames began, as a way of telling one person from another. So a redheaded person in Italy might have been nicknamed *Rosso*, which means "red" in Italian, and this turned into the surname "Rossi." Or a person in England who was always tired might have been nicknamed *Go to Bed*, which turned into the surname Gotobed. (Come on, Mr. Gotobed, just go to bed!) Back before the Middle Ages, your own surname might have started as a nickname like this.

Nowadays nicknames are often a shortening of part of a person's first name or surname, like *Dan* for *Dan*iel, or *Liz* for E*liz*abeth, or *Joe* for *Joseph*, or *Fito* for Adol*fito* (which is already a nickname for Adolfo). Sometimes the name changes a little, like James becomes *Jim*, and William *Bill*, or Katherine *Katie*.

Different languages have their own ways of making nicknames—in Taiwan, for example, children's nicknames are often made by repeating the first syllable of their name, so *Bozhi* turns into *Bobo*. In Spanish-speaking countries, often a person with green eyes will be nicknamed *Gato*, which means "cat." Do you know some other ways of making up nicknames?

Nicknames can also be kinds of jokes. In English, there's a tradition of giving someone a name that means the opposite of what they look like, so a bald man might be called *Curly*, or a tall person *Tiny*. This goes back a long way, and is almost a kind of euphemism. Remember *Little John*, one of Robin Hood's merry men in Sherwood Forest, who was actually really big?

Other joke nicknames might come from what a person does for a living, like a butcher might be called *Chops,* or an electrician *Sparky.* And can you work out why Mr. White is called *Chalky,* or Mrs. Fowler *Chick*?

Nicknames are everywhere—for politicians, for sports teams, even for buildings and countries. I'm sure you can think of many of these. (The Word Snoop is always happy to say she lives in the land of *Oz*!) You will have also used nicknames on the Internet, which are usually known as *handles* or *user names.*

Finally, there are the nicknames that tend to stick even if nobody remembers how they started or where they came from. The brilliant Brazilian football player Edson Arantes Do Nascimento, known all over the world by his nickname *Pelé,* does not know himself where the nickname began! This often happens in families when children are small. These can be the best sorts of nicknames—where they really belong to the person and make them feel loved. I wonder if you have some nicknames like that in your own family?

Eponyms

Know any good eponyms? No? Let's put it another way. Ever heard of *sideburns, salmonella,* or *sandwiches*? Ever been *mesmerized* or *mentored*? Do you know if *hooligans* have good *hygiene*?

What is the Word Snoop talking about?

All of these words are eponyms. An eponym is a word that comes from a person's name. *Epi* in Greek means "upon," and *onoma* means "name."

So all those words in italics came from names of either real or invented people, who said or did something memorable that meant something was named after them. Can you imagine the sort of hair the U.S. general Ambrose Everett *Burnside* had on his face? Or the disease Daniel *Salmon* was interested in? Or the Earl of *Sandwich*'s favorite food?

These are just a few eponyms, and you would know many more. Often it's just a matter of looking them up in a dictionary or on the Internet and finding the etymology of the word (which would tell you where the word originally came from). There are hundreds, probably thousands of eponyms in English, for all sorts of reasons. I wonder if you could find out where the names *Ferris* wheel came from, or *bloomers*, or *Granny Smith* apples (yum!), just to name a few.

It would be a strange thing, wouldn't it, to wake up in the morning and discover that something had been named after you? Hmm, in your case, I wonder what that would be? Or what you would *like* it to be?

As for me, I'd like to go to a restaurant and order myself a triple-chocolate-caramel-fudge-super-special *Word Snoop* . . .

FRANZ MESMER

Spoonerisms

Party time! Would you like a *belly jean?* No? What about a *chag* of *bips?* What on earth am I talking about? I'm playing a kind of word game called spoonerisms. Over 100 years ago at Oxford University in England, there was a man called the Reverend William Archibald Spooner. He was a gentle, white-haired history teacher, but that's not what he was famous for—it was the way he spoke that made everyone remember him.

Reverend Spooner had a funny habit of switching around the first letters of words near each other, which made them sound like different words altogether. So instead of saying "toe nails," for example, he might have said "*no* tails," instead of "blow your nose," he said "*kn*ow your *bl*ose." These are what we now call spoonerisms, after Reverend Spooner. (Aha! That's another eponym.)

Imagine if you had been one of Reverend Spooner's students, and he met you in the corridor. Can you work out what he's saying on the opposite page?

Student: Good morning, Reverend Spooner. How are you today?

Reverend Spooner: Wite quell, thank you. Dot are you wooing?

Student: Er, I've been playing football.

Reverend Spooner: Football! But you have hissed my mystery lecture!

Student: Oops.

Reverend Spooner: This is go nood. You've already tasted two worms playing football. Go and shake a tower and come straight to my office.

Student: Ses yer! I mean, yes sir.

Some people, like Reverend Spooner, can't help talking in spoonerisms, but that's very rare. Most of the time, writers and comedians make them up, for the fun of playing with words. I wonder if you can work out the spoonerisms on the next page? Better still, make up some really funny ones of your own!

Spoonerisms

1. It's roaring pain outside.
2. That's a lack of pies!
3. Would you like a soul of ballad?
4. I don't have time to chew my doors.
5. Do you live on this hock of blouses?
6. Eye ball!

Tom Swifties

You've heard of a cookie factory or an ice-cream factory, but imagine a writing factory! Rows and rows of writers hunched over desks writing story after story, trying to think up new plots and characters every day.

About 70 years ago in the United States, the E. L. Stratemeyer writing factory produced a popular series of children's adventure books about a boy genius inventor named Tom Swift. They had titles like *Tom Swift and His Sky Racer, Tom Swift and His Wizard Camera,* and *Tom Swift and His Giant Magnet.* These hardworking writers were teased for all the different words they used whenever Tom Swift said anything— Tom Swift didn't just say things, he *declared,* he *murmured,* he *whispered,* he *giggled,* he *stammered,* he *snorted,* he *sneered* . . . you get the idea!

Later, a kind of special joke developed out of this tendency of Tom's, called a *Tom Swifty*. It's a kind of pun, which is when you use a word that has two meanings at once to make people laugh. In a Tom Swifty, when Tom Swift says something, the writer uses a word that relates to what he is talking about to make a joke.

Like this:

"I just love cats," Tom Swift purred.
(Cats purr, get it?)

"I checked, and there really are 432,911 lollipops in the jar," Tom Swift recounted. (Tom counted the lollpops again, and then he told you about it!)

Then there's another type of Tom Swifty where it's the adverb (which is the word that tells you *how* he says something) that makes the joke. Take a look at the ones on the following page.

> "Who turned out the lights?" Tom Swift said darkly.
>
> "Can you lend me your pencil sharpener?" asked Tom Swift bluntly.
>
> "Would you like to pet my cocker spaniel?" Tom Swift suggested doggedly.
>
> "I'm no good at darts," Tom Swift said aimlessly.

Try to make some up yourself. Once you start, it can be hard to stop (said the Word Snoop *open-endedly . . .*).

Malapropisms

*"My favorite dessert is chocolate mouse
with decimated coconut."*

Now, there's something not quite right here.
The person speaking has got some words and
expressions a bit mixed up. This is called a malapropism. A malapropism is when you confuse
words that may seem or sound similar, but have
different meanings. So here the person probably
meant that chocolate *mousse* was their favorite
dessert, and they liked to eat it with *desiccated*
coconut.

Like *spoonerism* and *Tom Swifty*, the word
malapropism is an eponym named after a person,
in this case Mrs. Malaprop. She wasn't a real person, but a character in a play called *The Rivals*,
written by Irish playwright Richard Sheridan in
1775. He gave her the name Mrs. Malaprop from
a French phrase *mal à propos*, which means "not
quite right." If you ever get to see *The Rivals*, you
will find yourself laughing and laughing. (The
Word Snoop had to leave the theater and get
herself a large glass of water, she was laughing so

much.) It's not because of anything Mrs. Mala-prop does, but the things she says. For example, she compares someone to an *allegory* on the Nile instead of an *alligator,* and even describes some-one as "the very *pineapple* of politeness." (Um, I think that should be *pinnacle,* Mrs. M!)

Of course, malapropisms existed long before Mrs. Malaprop appeared. Sometimes they are called *Dogberryisms* after a sort of policeman character called Dogberry who made the same sorts of mistakes as Mrs. Malaprop—and Dogberry appeared in a play by William Shakespeare that was written almost 200 years before *The Rivals.*

Malapropisms have been around as long as people have been speaking and writing and making mistakes (as we all do from time to time). They're often found in the conversations of small children, who hear lots of new words each day. Sally Brown from Charles Schulz's cartoon strip *Peanuts* talks about some cavemen who are "suddenly attacked by a huge *thesaurus*"; and the babies in the television cartoon *Rugrats* say things like: "Somebody got up on the wrong side of the *bread*" and "For *feet's* sake!"

But Mrs. Malaprop's spirit lives on in grown-ups, too. Dorrie Evans, a favorite character in the long-running 1970s Australian soap opera *Number 96,* was a kind of modern-day Mrs. Malaprop, with remarks like: "Pardon me for *protruding*" (intruding) and "Life is not a bowl of *cherubs*" (cherries). And in the TV comedy *Kath and Kim,* both mother and daughter are constantly coming out with things like: "I don't want to be rich. I want to be *effluent*" (affluent), or "The ozone diet? What does that *pacifically* (specifically) entail?" In fact, they are so well-known for this you will now sometimes find malapropisms called *Kath and Kimisms*.

What makes malapropisms so funny? Well, the Austrian psychoanalyst Dr. Sigmund Freud believed that the mistakes we make in speech (sometimes known as "Freudian slips") tell us a lot of truth about ourselves—more, in fact, than when we say everything correctly. So perhaps we laugh because we are shocked by the sudden truths a malapropism reveals . . .

Hmm. Next time you write a story or a play, why not try livening it up with a few malapropisms? In the meantime, see if you can work out what's not quite right about the sentences on the following page.

Malapropisms

1. An amphibious person can write with both hands.
2. Stop being such an idiom!
3. She was rushed to the hospital with a bad case of ammonia.
4. The old man with gray hair looked very extinguished.

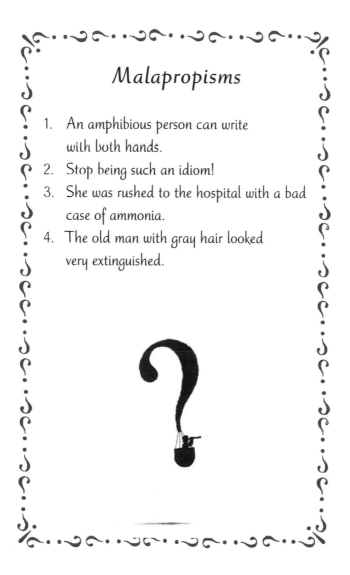

Pen Names

Have you ever read a book by Theodor Geisel? No? I bet you have. I'll give you a hint, there's this story about a cat with a hat . . .

Aha! Of course—Dr. Seuss. But *Dr. Seuss* wasn't the name he was born with. It was his pen name, a name a person uses when he publishes a book. This is also known as a *pseudonym,* Greek for "false name," or a *nom de plume,* which is French for "name of pen." In Theodor Geisel's case, Seuss was his middle name. He began using it when he was a young man, drawing and writing for a university magazine. Later, he added the "Dr." for fun, in honor of the doctoral degree he never managed to get at the university.

So why didn't he just use his own name in the first place? Well, sometimes writers want to use a different name for different kinds of writing. The mathematics professor Charles Lutwidge Dodgson used the pen name Lewis Carroll when he wrote *Alice's Adventures in Wonderland,* because he wanted to keep his real name for his books about mathematics and philosophy. It was the same for Daniel Handler, a writer for adults, when he decided to use a pen name for his series of unfortunately eventful children's books. You know who I mean . . . *Lemony Snicket.*

There can be all sorts of other reasons for using a pen name. The French novelist Albert Camus, who won the Nobel Prize for literature, wrote under the pen name Bauchard during World War II to trick his enemies. The Irish writer Oscar Wilde used the name Sebastian Melmoth after he came out of prison, because he thought that people might be prejudiced against him. And the playwright Molière took on this one-word name so his family wouldn't be embarrassed (in those days people didn't think the theater was a respectable place to work). His real name was Jean-Baptiste Poquelin.

Some female writers have written under pen names too, either because they wanted to keep their privacy, or because they were afraid that people didn't think women should write books. This happened a lot in the nineteenth century. Jane Austen, the author of *Pride and Prejudice,* wrote all her novels anonymously, without any name on them at all. (Now that's shy!) And one of the greatest writers of the nineteenth century, George

Eliot, was actually a woman named Mary Ann Evans. The wonderful Australian novelist Henry Handel Richardson was really named Ethel Richardson, just as fellow writer Miles Franklin's real first name was Stella.

It can work the other way as well—a man might choose to write under a woman's name. The author of *The Wizard of Oz*, L. Frank Baum, also used the names Laura Bandcroft and Edith Van Dyne. He must have wondered exactly who he was sometimes . . .

It's not surprising, when you think about it, that authors like to use pen names. After all, it comes naturally to a writer to make up characters. It's fun and exciting to become another person for a while—like being an undercover agent! The Danish philosopher Søren Kierkegaard sometimes signed his books *John of Silence*. Hmm, that gets me thinking. How about *Elspeth of Imagination* or *Ali the Ambidextrous* or . . .

What pen name would you use, snoops? You could try using an anagram of your own name. That's what the inventor of the telephone, Alexander Graham Bell, did—he wrote articles under the name H. A. Largelamb, a pen name he made up for himself as a child. Or you could just let your imagination go wild! Here are a few nutty pen names of some very respectable authors, just to give you some ideas.

Michael Angelo Titmarsh
C. J. Yellowplush, Esq.
Miss Tickletoby
(Real name: William Makepeace Thackeray, author of *Vanity Fair*)

Malachi Malagrowther
Captain Clutterbuck
Crystal Croftangry
(Real name: Sir Walter Scott, author of *Ivanhoe*)

Isaac Bickerstaff
A. Dissenter
M. B. Drapier
(Real name: Jonathan Swift, author of *Gulliver's Travels*)

Hmm, *the Word Snoop*. Do you think that could possibly be a pen name . . . ?

Uh-oh, Word Snoops, we're up to the second to the last code! (Will you miss them when they're gone?) See how quickly you can figure this one out. (Hint: How well can you count?)

WHO AM I?
MY FIRST IS IN WALRUS
MY SECOND IS IN DOLPHIN
MY THIRD IS IN PORCUPINE
MY FOURTH IS IN GANDER
MY FIFTH IS IN GOATS
MY SIXTH IS IN PIT-PONY
MY SEVENTH AND EIGHTH ARE IN COCKATOO
MY NINTH IS IN RED SHRIMP

Answers

SPOONERISMS

1. It's pouring rain outside.
2. That's a pack of lies!
3. Would you like a bowl of salad?
4. I don't have time to do my chores.
5. Do you live on this block of houses?
6. Bye all!

MALAPROPISMS

1. An ambidextrous person can write with both hands.
2. Stop being such an idiot!
3. She was rushed to the hospital with a bad case of pneumonia.
4. The old man with gray hair looked very distinguished.

Dear Snoops,

We are now coming to the end of
this book (phew!) and (sob!).

By now you will have noticed that many of the
words we've been snooping on together are very
old—even thousands of years old. But this last
adventure into the world of texting and Internet
languages is far newer—or is it?

Probably by the time this book is published,
some of the things I'm going to write about here
will no longer be true. That's how it is with
words. As soon as you think you understand
what's going on, it all changes. Words jump and
run and cartwheel around like a gang of spider
monkeys. You can hardly keep your eye on one
before another one is leaping around and doing
something different altogether.

But U kp rdn itz bn gr8!

Da Werd Snewp

10.
Back
to the
future

Telegramese

First, to go back in time . . .

I know, I know—I said this was going to be about new things. But there's just a little bit of history to begin with.

Many years ago (like more than 100), there were no such things as texts or e-mail or even the telephone. If you wanted to send someone far away a short message very fast, you had to put a letter in an empty bottle and throw it in the ocean . . .

Ha ha! Only joking. :-)

I'll start that again. If you wanted to send someone far away a short message very fast *electronically,* you had to use something called a telegram. This was usually done at the post office. You would tell the person at the post office what you wanted to say and they would type it into a machine, which would send the message electronically to another post office anywhere in the world.

Now, in a telegram you paid for each word,

so to save money you used as few words as possible. As a result, a very short way of saying things developed, known as telegramese. In some ways it was like the brief writing we use in mobile phone text messages today. Have a look at this telegram that the Word Snoop's great-grandmother received on her 113th birthday, from her favorite grandson, Alyosha:

HAPPY 113 GRANNY STOP HOPE CAKE
YUMMY STOP LEAVE ME SOME OR ELSE
STOP LOVE ALWAYS ALYOSHA

Just like in a text message, you can see that Alyosha tried to keep the message short by leaving out words he might have put in if he'd been writing a letter. You can also see that, unlike text messages, telegrams were printed in CAPITAL LETTERS, which meant it looked like you were SHOUTING, and the word STOP was used for a period. You could include other punctuation if you wanted to, but a single mark cost the same as a single word, so people rarely did.

Okay, so both telegrams and text messages are short, but the big difference between the two is that millions of texts are sent around the world every day, whereas telegrams were mainly kept for special occasions. This meant that unlike the ever-changing, ever-developing language of texting, telegramese remained pretty much the same.

It's funny—even though nowadays with the Internet and mobile phones there's no real need for telegrams anymore, people still seem to like them and you can still send a telegram from the post office if you want to.

Or a gorillagram if you *really* want to . . .

Singing telegrams

When telegrams began 100 years ago, they were mainly used to communicate bad news—that is, to say that someone was sick or had died. So when the telegram boy arrived at the door, most people thought "Uh-oh." To encourage people to think of telegrams as happy things, singing telegrams were invented in the 1930s. A delivery boy would come to your door and sing a message, usually for someone's birthday or a wedding.

It must have been quite hard sometimes. Try singing this telegram that Alyosha got back in reply from my great-grandmother:

CAT ATE CAKE STOP NONE LEFT
STOP HARD CHEESE SONNY STOP
MAYBE NEXT YEAR STOP HA HA
STOP LOVE ALWAYS GRANNY

Texting, LOL, Leet and More

HOW R U
I R OK HOW BOUT U
:-)
THTZ GUD 2NO CU L8TR

Can you read this? If you send a lot of text messages through your mobile phone, I'm sure you can. If not, it probably looks pretty peculiar. Many people (well, let's face it, adults) look at text messages and think: "Hey, these kids don't know how to spell or write." But it's a lot more inventive than that.

The words in text messages have a lot in common with the words you find in Internet slang and Internet languages, like LOL (Laugh Out Loud) or Leet, or other ways people communicate through the computer or game consoles.

Although it seems very new and modern, quite a lot of the tricks of this sort of writing have actually been around for years—centuries, even. Have a look for yourself:

* leaving out vowels (a, e, i, o, u), like **bn** for "been" or **fst** for "fast." Well, remember originally the alphabet had no vowels.

* changed or shortened spelling, usually so the word is written as it's spoken, like **cud** for "could" or **vzt** for "visit." People have been wanting to change spelling like this for ages.

* using little punctuation and few capital letters, like **wnt 2 go 4 pza**. Well, in the beginning English didn't use either of these things anyway.

* using numbers or letters that sound like words instead of the word itself. So **B4** for "before" or **L8** for "late," **CU** for "see you." That's something as old as the hills—remember the rebus?

* acronyms, like **ttyl** for "talk to you later" or **bff** for "best friends forever." Even the ancient Romans used acronyms.

* clipping words, either at the beginning, like **lo** for "hello," or at the end, like **rad** for "radical." We all use plenty of words like this already—just think of **bus** for "omnibus" or **pop** for "popular."

* deliberate mistakes, like changing the grammar to make the text shorter, like **i r** for "I am"; or typing "own" as **pwn** on purpose, instead of by accident.

So as you can see, it's the technology, the *way* the messages are sent, rather than the language that makes it so new. But it has given rise to some new forms of writing. Text poetry, for example. After all, the shortness of text messages calls for very concentrated ideas and images, rather like the traditional Haiku poetry of Japan. Works of Shakespeare and Dickens and even the Lord's Prayer have all been turned into text language. And now novels written entirely in instant messaging have started to appear, such as *ttyl* and *ttfn* by Lauren Myracle—maybe you can find them in the library. Or why not try writing a text story or poem yourself?

In the meantime, can you work out what popular folk song the Word Snoop has "translated" into text?

Twinkle, twinkle ltl (*),
how I 1Dr wot U R. ^ abof d wrld so hI,
lIk a diamond n d sky.
Twinkle, twinkle ltl (*),
how I 1Dr wot U R.

Smileys

I'm sad to say we're almost at the end of this book. But I'm glad to say we're finishing with something happy—smileys. (See, you're smiling already!)

A smiley is a symbol you create by using the punctuation marks on the keyboard to make messages without words. The most common is the happy face ("smiley," get it?) made up of a colon and a bracket. It looks like eyes and a smiling mouth if you turn your head sideways (don't hurt your neck . . .).

:]

Some people like to put in a hyphen for the nose.

:-]

Okay, turn your head back the right way now.

The smiley started off in e-mails, to show that something was a joke (or at least not meant to be taken too seriously). Some people find that it's hard to express emotions in written words alone, and so a smiley can take the place of tone of voice or the look on a face. If you got a message like this, for example:

PLZ COME NOW

you might think the person was saying crossly,

"'Get here at once!" whereas what they really wanted to say was:

PLZ COME NOW :)

In other words, "Pretty please, I really really want you to come over now, pleeeeeease."

The happy face was just the beginning—very quickly dozens of other symbols started appearing, like:

a wink: **;)**

a blush: **:*)**

a frownie: **:(**

They're all generally called smileys (or sometimes *emoticons*), even if they're not smiling. Look on the Internet—you'll find hundreds of them, as many as there are human feelings. There are different ones for different languages, and new ones being made up all the time. You've probably made up a few yourselves!

Half the fun is making them up, and the

other half is trying to interpret them, to understand what they mean. Here, have a quick smiley test—what do you think these could mean?

:O

:X

>:(

Well, now that we've come to the end of the book, I suppose it could mean that I'm *surprised,* or want to *kiss* you, or that I'm very very *angry,* but really I'm just:

crying because the time has come to say . . .

Adieu! from the Word Snoop . . .

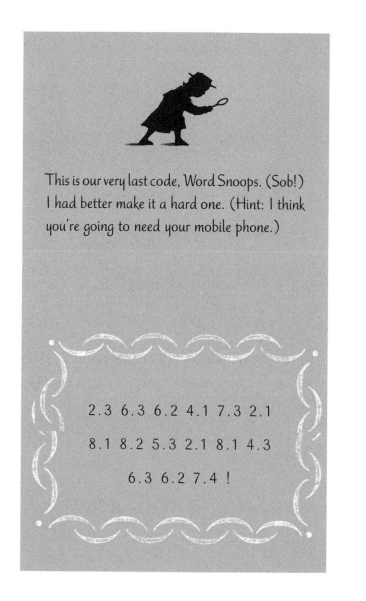

This is our very last code, Word Snoops. (Sob!)
I had better make it a hard one. (Hint: I think
you're going to need your mobile phone.)

2.3 6.3 6.2 4.1 7.3 2.1

8.1 8.2 5.3 2.1 8.1 4.3

6.3 6.2 7.4 !

Dear Snoops,

This really is now the end of the book and the end of my secrets (not ALL my secrets, mind you, but quite a few of them). Just think of all the strange things we've explored together on the way. From anagrams and acronyms to tautologies and tongue twisters, eponyms and exclamation marks—and our journey has really only just begun. There are so many astonishing things to discover about words, I don't think you could ever come to the end of the secrets they hold.

My dear snoops, I've had a wonderful time with you all. But I've been sitting at my desk typing away for so long, I'm eager to travel forth again into the wonderful wordy world and make some new discoveries!

I hope we will meet again. I'm sure we will.

Would you recognize me, though, if you saw me? I wonder…

In the meantime, keep brave! Keep bright! Keep snooping! Yours ever,

The Word Snoop

Word Snoop Glossary

Acronym—a word formed by using the beginning letters of other words. For example, CD for Compact Disc, or SCUBA for Self-Contained Underwater Breathing Apparatus.

Alphabet—letters or signs of a language that represent sounds

Anagram—a word formed by mixing up the letters of another word. For example, tale is an anagram of late.

Backronym—when the letters of a well-known word are used to make up a sentence. Sometimes this sentence reflects what the word actually means. For example, FEAR—Forget Everything And Run!

Circumlocution—using so many words to say something, it can be hard to work out what is actually being said

Cliché—a well-known expression that has been used so often that it no longer carries as much meaning as it did originally. For example, quiet as a mouse.

Doublespeak—using vague words and indirect expressions to hide the truth

Eponym—a word that is based on the name of a person. For example, *braille* after the French teacher Louis Braille, who invented the system.

Etymology—the study of the history of words and their meanings

Euphemism—indirect words and expressions used for things that are embarrassing or unpleasant to say. For example, *the ladies' room* for "toilet" and *kick the bucket* for "die."

Homophones—two words that sound the same but have different meanings and often different spellings. For example, *rows* and *rose*.

Leet—(short for *elite*) a kind of Internet and gaming slang that uses a lot of numbers

Lipogram—a piece of writing in which the author deliberately leaves out a specific letter of the alphabet

LOL—(short for Laugh Out Loud) an Internet slang language that uses many of the features found in texting. For example, using acronyms and numbers instead of letters, and deliberate misspellings such as woz for was.

Malapropism—misusing words or expressions in a way that is funny. For example, Aunt Artica for *Antarctica*.

Mnemonics—tricks and techniques that people use to help them remember things. For example, the sentence Every Good Boy Deserves Fruit helps people remember the order of the notes on a music stave: E G B D F.

Mondegreen—a word or phrase that is misheard, usually from song lyrics. For example, "When a man loves a walnut" instead of "When a man loves a woman."

Nickname—an extra name for someone or something, which is usually affectionate and often funny

Onomatopoeia—words that suggest the sound something makes. For example, *woof* for the barking of a dog.

Oronyms—phrases that sound the same but are spelled differently and have different meanings. For example, "ice cream" and "I scream." Note, generally the word *homophone* is used to describe one of a pair of words that have the same sound ("allowed" and "aloud"), while *oronym* refers to strings of words or phrases ("iced ink" and "I stink").

Oxymoron—an expression that seems to contradict itself. For example, it was freezing hot!

Palindrome—a word or phrase that reads the same backward as forward. For example, radar.

Pangram—a sentence that uses every letter in the alphabet

Pen name—a false or extra name taken on by a writer instead of their real name

Pig Latin—one of many playful ways of making ordinary language hard for others to understand, by adding extra sounds. For example, Ave-hay ou-yay et-may e-thay Ord-way Noop-say?

Portmanteau word—a word made up by putting two different words together, and usually losing a bit of each word. For example, *blog* for "web" and "log."

Punctuation—a system of symbols that are added to written words to show meaning

Pun—purposely using a word with two meanings, usually to make a joke. For example: Why won't a circus lion eat the clowns? Because they taste funny.

Rebus—using pictures or symbols to represent words or sounds

Rhyming slang—replacing a word or phrase with a rhyming word or phrase. For example, *wooden pegs* for "legs."

Silent letter—a letter in a word that is not pronounced. For example, the *k* in *knock*.

Smileys—signs made from punctuation marks used in e-mails and text messages to show emotions, like happiness :-). Also called emoticons.

Spoonerism—mixing up the sounds of words with a funny effect. For example, "wave the sails" for "save the whales."

Tautology—saying the same thing twice in one expression. For example, smelly aroma.

Telegramese—a very short way of writing used in telegrams, which are an old form of electronic communication

Texting—a message sent through a mobile phone

Tom Swifty—a kind of pun, named after a book character called Tom Swift, where a word is used to describe someone's dialogue in a clever way. For example, "Don't you like snakes?" hissed Tom.

Tongue twister—a phrase that is very hard to say because of the repetition of similar sounds. For example, Six thick thistle sticks.

The Keys to the Word Snoop's Codes

Hello, Word Snoops. How did you do with all those codes? Did you decipher my message?

Hmm, maybe some of the codes were a bit too tricky. Well, in that case, here are some keys that will help you unlock the codes and work out the message, just like opening a locked door and finding what's inside . . .

So go on, snoops—have another go!

CHAPTER ONE
Key
ABCDEFGHIJKLMNOPQRSTUVWXYZ
ZYXWVUTSRQPONMLKJIHGFEDCBA
So A = Z   B = Y etc.

CHAPTER TWO
Key
Adding a silent letter to every second letter
So "hakrdkly" = hardly

CHAPTER THREE
Key
! @ # $ % ^ & * ( ) _ + { } [ ] : " ; ' < > ? , . /
A B C D E F G H I J K L M N O P Q R S T U V W X Y Z
So A = !, B = @ etc.

CHAPTER FOUR
Key
A vital letter is left out
So "Ould you ome to the akeshop for a upake?" =
Could you come to the cakeshop for a cupcake?

CHAPTER FIVE
Key
A backward code
So "drawkcab nettirw si egassem siht" =
this message is written backward

CHAPTER SIX
Key
A rebus code
So "ACDEFG" = Begone! ("B" gone—get it?)

CHAPTER SEVEN
Key
A "say it out loud" code
So "Kan ute rye took rack thee scoad?" =
Can you try to crack this code?

CHAPTER EIGHT
Key
A first letter code
So "Better Eaten When Ants Rushing Everywhere" =
BEWARE

CHAPTER NINE
Key
A numbered letter code
So: My first is in strawberries
My second is in snow pea
My third and fourth are in blood oranges
My fifth is in bosc-pear
My sixth is in grapes
= snoops

CHAPTER TEN

Key

A mobile phone code related to the numbers you
would press if you were texting

So A = 2.1 (press the "2" key once)

B = 2.2 (press the "2" key twice)

C = 2.3 (press the "2" key three times)

etc.

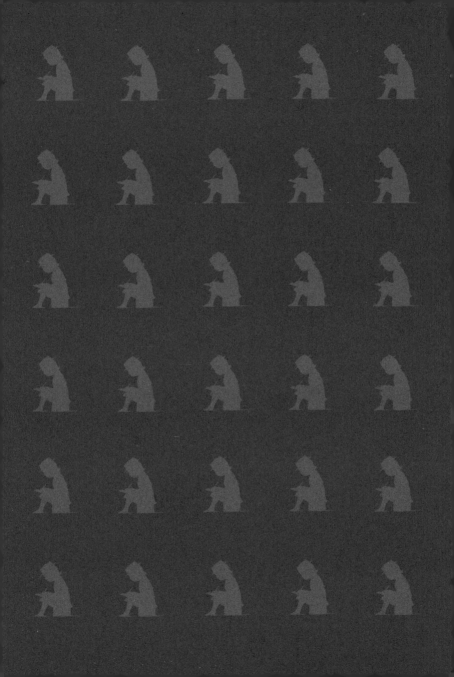